the POWER of ALL

"This is not an easier way to do church, just a more biblical and fruitful way. With eyes open to opportunities and pitfalls, the authors give inspiring rationale and wise counsel for a church where everyone contributes."
—J. Nelson Kraybill, pastor, president emeritus of Anabaptist Mennonite Biblical Seminary, Elkhart, Indiana

"Most churches have lost sight of the biblical vision of being multivoiced and have sunk into performance/audience mode. This book not only renews that biblical vision but also provides many glimpses of what it can mean in practice today."
—Jeremy Thomson, principal lecturer in theology at Oasis College, United Kingdom

"Sian and Stuart Murray Williams draw on a wealth of experience in this impassioned plea for the revival of a multivoiced approach to being church and engaging in worship. If their argument is heeded it will help people in the churches to grow in their discipleship and their engagement with the world."
—Stephen Finamore, principal of Bristol Baptist College, United Kingdom

"The church in North America faces a stark choice: transformation or extinction. The road to transformation involves re-establishing relational discipleship in the church over institutional programming by the church. Stuart and Sian Murray Williams have offered us a compelling vision for being the church."
—Jeff Wright, pastor, missional strategist with Urban Expression North America, Riverside, California

the POWER *of* ALL
Building a Multivoiced Church

Sian and Stuart Murray Williams

Herald Press
Harrisonburg, Virginia
Waterloo, Ontario

Library of Congress Cataloging-in-Publication Data
Williams, Sian Murray, 1960-
The power of all : building a multivoiced church / Sian and Stuart Murray Williams.
    p. cm.
    ISBN 978-0-8361-9643-6 (pbk.)
    1. Church and minorities. 2. Multiculturalism—Religious aspects—Christianity.
3. Social integration—Religious aspects—Christianity. 4. Ethnicity—Religious
aspects—Christianity. 5. Christianity and culture. I. Murray, Stuart, 1956- II. Title.
    BV639.M56W56 2012
    262—dc23
                                                                    2012017819

This North American edition of *The Power of All* is based on *Multi-Voiced Church*, first published in 2012 by Paternoster, an imprint of Authentic, 52 Presley Way, Crownhill, Milton Keynes, MK8 0ES, U.K. This edition is published by agreement with Paternoster. In relation to the UK edition, the right of Stuart and Sian Murray Williams to be identified as the Author of this Work has been asserted by them in accordance with the Copyright, Designs, and Patents Act 1988.

THE POWER OF ALL
Copyright © 2012 by Herald Press, Harrisonburg, Virginia 22802
    Released simultaneously in Canada by Herald Press,
    Waterloo, Ontario N2L 6H7. All rights reserved.
Library of Congress Control Number: 2012017819
International Standard Book Number: 978-0-8361-9643-6
Printed in United States of America
Cover design by Reuben Graham

16 15 14 13 12   10 9 8 7 6 5 4 3 2 1

To order or request information, please call 1-800-245-7894 in the U.S. or
1-800-631-6535 in Canada. Or visit www.heraldpress.com.

With grateful thanks to our parents
Gwyndaf and Betty Williams
Norman and Hazel Murray

Contents

Foreword

At a recent conference in Sydney on mission-focused churches, the speaker launched the gathering with the provocative lines "Most Christians are not engaged as participants in the mission of God" and "Churches have structured for passivity!"[1] I visit a lot of very different churches, and I have to say that increasingly the Sunday worship experience is a very passive affair for the majority of attendees.

Often the auditorium is darkened so that all the focus is on the stage, which implicitly reinforces that we are present at a performance. It is not a big step from there to the notion that we come to church to be entertained and inspired by specialists. The people at the front assist us in worshiping in our private space and may well helpfully encourage us to live better for Christ in the week, but I will have contributed nothing other than my body heat to the experience. The structure does indeed seem to enable passivity. This seems a long way from the pattern we see in the early churches of everyone using their gifts and bringing something to offer when the body gathers. What has happened over the last thirty odd years that has moved us from the emphasis on "body ministry" to where we are today?

---

1. Ed Stetzer at the Ten Conference at Small Boat Big Sea (a church community in Sydney) celebrating ten years of "making a difference."

The Murray Williamses argue that multivoiced participation has always been at its highest during a renewal movement and then lapses in the intervening years. Specialist-led church is thus a sign of church decline—a desperate substitution of professionalism for collective passion. This book is therefore a timely reminder that, in striving to reinvigorate a struggling church and recover a mission focus, we may be barking up the wrong tree. Rather than keep improving the quality of the music and presentation at the front, maybe we need to start re-enfranchising the congregation and empowering them to have a voice and make an offering.

The Power of All is an antidote to the boredom many experience in church, and also to the growing irregularity of attendance. "What difference does it make if I am not there? The band will still go on singing and the preacher will preach, so no one will miss me!" Sian and Stuart have written a very practical book with plenty of ideas about doing church differently—not just changing the worship service, but also looking at the way we build community and make decisions together. These practical suggestions are firmly supported by a biblical framework, and also address many of the realities of making the transition and dealing with the inevitable messiness of change.

Having read the manuscript of this book, I was inspired to rewrite a sermon for a pastor's induction; to cut it down considerably and make space for small groups to engage with the text and produce from it their own hopes, dreams, and blessings for their new pastor, and he for them. What would have been a safe, predictable, and probably unmemorable (albeit adequately inspiring!) monologue became an occasion when the community of all ages and nationalities participated movingly in multivoiced benediction.

I reckon that new action in response to a book must be every Christian author's delight, and I know Sian and Stuart well enough to recognize that this is their motivation for writing *The Power of All*. They have not written a book to pump up their own egos or fill out their already impressive CVs; rather, they both deeply desire that the church be transformed for mission in today's post-Christendom context. *The Power of All* is an important book for all churches in the more affluent parts of the globe at this time of liminality and change.

Many churches are struggling to keep pace with population growth, and many are actively declining in numbers. In this book we are encouraged to arrest that trajectory, not by following the trends of celebrity-led culture, but by practicing biblical patterns of community life. This is a book that offers hope particularly to the smaller churches, because they are often best placed to encourage everyone to make an offering and most easily enable everyone to have a voice. The path to change, to renewed mission and social transformation, is simply to rediscover the gifts that the Spirit has given to every believer and offer ways for them to be expressed. This isn't a new message, but it appears to be a lost message that needs recovering.

This is a book that will greatly assist anyone who sits in church and occasionally wonders why they bother! It is a book for church leaders and pastors who feel frustrated and exhausted by the demands to "do church better" for their congregation. It is a book for people who want to recover something authentic, biblical, and connected with others in their faith journey. It is a book that we need to read and pass on to others. It is a book we need to act on.

Anne Wilkinson-Hayes
Acting Director of Ministries,
Baptist Union of Victoria, Australia

Preface

We first encountered the term *multivoiced church* many years ago in conversation with Eleanor Kreider. In her book *Enter His Gates*,[1] Eleanor explores what this means for the worshiping life of Christian communities. And in the more recent *Worship and Mission After Christendom*,[2] written jointly with her husband, Alan, there are many resources for communities wanting to explore this approach to church life. We gratefully acknowledge the influence of these dear friends on our thinking and practice.

The term *multivoiced* also appears in the core convictions of the Anabaptist Network,[3] which Stuart has chaired for several years. Discerning readers will undoubtedly recognize the influence of that tradition in this book, and we introduce Anabaptism in Chapter 3 as an example of a multivoiced renewal movement. And we write as Baptists (Sian teaches at a Baptist college and is a Baptist minister) and acknowledge that many of the examples we use and stories we share come from churches in this or other free church traditions.

---

1. Eleanor Kreider, *Enter His Gates: Fitting Worship Together* (Basingstoke: Marshall Pickering, 1992).

2. Alan Kreider and Eleanor Kreider, *Worship and Mission After Christendom* (Harrisonburg: Herald Press, 2011).

3. See www.anabaptistnetwork.com.

But we have both valued interaction with other Christian traditions and we hope that what we have written will be accessible more widely, perhaps with some necessary translation. For readers in some emerging churches or older charismatic churches, some of what we have written will probably seem too institutional; readers from churches in the liturgical and sacramental traditions may find some of it lightweight or irresponsible. But we hope at least some of the material we present and resources we offer will be helpful in these contexts, too.

This is the first book we have written together (an interesting experience), but we have taught together on this and other topics. In fact, it was at a conference in June 2008 for newly accredited Baptist ministers that we presented material we are drawing on here and several people encouraged us to write a book on the subject. As we reflected on this we decided, not only that we should write together (a monovoiced approach would hardly be appropriate), but also that we would invite others to contribute stories and insights. We are grateful to those who have responded to this invitation: Ben Lucas; Trevor Neill; Ken Adolphe; Karen Stallard; Brian Haymes; Angie Tunstall; Jonny Baker; Tim Presswood; Jeremy Thomson; Ali Boulton; Trevor Withers; Marg Hardcastle; Jenni Entrican; Matt and Jules Hollidge; Tim Foley; Susan Williams; Phil Warburton; Phill Vickery; Trisha Dale, Littlemore Baptist Church, Oxford; and several members of Wood Green Mennonite Church in London.

1

What Is Multivoiced Church?

Multivoiced church in action

Rather than starting with a definition, let's begin with some snapshots of multivoiced church in action.

When the band was away

One Sunday in mid-August, in an inner-city Baptist church, all the worship leaders and musicians were on holiday. The church member responsible for leading the service read out 1 Corinthians 14:26: "When you come together, everyone has a hymn, or a word of instruction, a revelation, a tongue, or an interpretation. All of these must be done for the strengthening of the church." He suggested the congregation take this seriously and saw the absent musicians as an opportunity, not a problem. For the next thirty minutes it was hard to get a word in as many voices were raised in praise and prayer, bringing words of encouragement, reading biblical passages, and leading in unaccompanied singing. Maybe this wasn't surprising. For several years this congregation had had no musicians, but new people joining had meant a worship band could be formed and worship leaders chosen. The church was grateful for the band and the worship leaders, but on this Sunday multivoiced church reemerged.

When the minister was off sick

He had been the minister of this suburban Baptist church for several years and was loved and appreciated. Then he was signed off by his doctor for a stress-related illness, and this period away from the church went on for several months. Only then did the church realize how utterly dependent they had become on him. He did everything. Every decision went through him. He took all the initiatives. Church members had been disempowered and had become passive. It was not easy, but gradually they learned to take responsibility for their church and its mission. But it had taken a crisis to subvert the monovoiced church.

When a new church is forming

Ali Boulton is planting a church on a new housing estate in Swindon, UK. She writes:

> Being multivoiced is an intrinsic part of who we are. We are a small-ish gathering of up to thirty people of mixed ages (at least one person born in each decade from the current one back to the 1940s), the majority being unchurched new Christians or people exploring faith, with a wide social demographic, including a large part of the group on benefits. We meet at my house for lunch and then explore faith and worship together. The size, venue, demographic, and unchurched culture all contribute to a multivoiced gathering. People speak up, ask questions, and contribute in an unplanned, informal way as well as taking part in discussions, leading or choosing songs, contributing to liturgy and prayer, or leading part of the gathering in a more corporately agreed way. The children and adults are involved in storytelling, and we have a dressing-up box which facilitates our scratch dramas, which generally people love. Being multivoiced is who/what we are. We wouldn't want to be any other way.

When church is messy

One of the most popular "fresh expressions" of church in recent years has been "Messy Church," pioneered by Lucy Moore and adopted in many different contexts. For those who are unfamiliar with this model, it involves all-age activities, creativity, hospitality, and celebration. Reflecting on his visits to a number of these communities, George Lings notes that a key component is participation. Instead of being choreographed by texts and pre-chosen PowerPoint slides, all the participants are actively involved in making church happen. He comments approvingly that this is "turning being church back into a creative, participatory, communal hive of spiritual life."[1]

Rediscovering multivoiced church

A recurring feature of renewal movements in the history of the church is their multivoiced nature. No longer is the Christian community largely passive, dependent on a few authorized ministers to preach, conduct worship, provide pastoral care, engage in mission, and exercise leadership. Men and women, young and old, educated and illiterate, rich and poor find their voices and discover their vocations. The ancient prophecy of Joel, fulfilled dramatically on the day of Pentecost—"I will pour out my Spirit on all people"[2]—comes alive again in first-generation movements across the globe and through the centuries.

For those who have only known monovoiced church, multivoiced church is liberating, empowering, exciting, dynamic, and energizing. What was monochrome has suddenly become multicolored. Soloists have been engulfed by a full orchestra. But those caught up in these movements often struggle to know how to prevent the many voices from becoming a cacophony, how to channel the energies that have been released into effective mission and ministry, how to weigh diverse contributions and discern the authentic voice of the Spirit. Sometimes the enthusiasm and freedom result in chaos and pain.

This scenario is as old as the New Testament. In 1 Corinthians 14 (a favorite passage in multivoiced renewal movements), the

---

1. George Lings, "Messy Church," *Encounters on the Edge, no. 46* (Sheffield: The Sheffield Centre, 2010), 8. See further Lucy Moore, *Messy Church* (Oxford: Bible Reading Fellowship, 2006).

2. Joel 2:28, quoted in Acts 2:17.

apostle Paul provides guidance for a multivoiced church. He does not want to restrict their freedom or still the many voices, but he wants all they do to build up the community, present a positive witness to outsiders, and honor God. Multivoiced church, if it is to flourish, needs to develop good habits and practices.

But very often multivoiced church does not survive past the first or second generation of renewal movements. Internal struggles, criticism from others, and the powerful influence of the much more familiar monovoiced tradition take their toll and gradually the default position is reestablished. Formalized vestiges of the multivoiced practices may remain, but the vibrancy of a truly multivoiced community has gone—until it is rediscovered by the next renewal movement.

The case for multivoiced church

We write with the conviction that multivoiced church is normative (if not normal) and a healthier form of church than the monovoiced alternative that has been dominant over the centuries. We gratefully acknowledge all that we ourselves, and many others, have learned and received from monovoiced churches. But we believe multivoiced church equips the Christian community for mission, stimulates personal growth, encourages responsible discipleship, protects the community from many ills, and allows God's Spirit freedom to accomplish so much more in and through the church.

We recognize that we may be addressing readers whose initial response to this conviction can be summarized in one of the following ways:

- Multivoiced church is uncongenial and unthinkable. This may be the reaction of those with a sacramental and priestly view of ministry, those who look to apostles and elders to direct the affairs of the church, and those whose culture predisposes them to expect the pastor to do all the preaching, lead all the services, provide all the pastoral care, and make all the decisions.

- Multivoiced church is natural and normal. This may be the perspective of those who belong to some of the newer churches that have been emerging over recent years, especially those which meet in homes and encourage the multiplication of simple and participatory expressions of church.

- Multivoiced church is partial and sporadic. This may be the experience of those who are members of congregations from various denominations and traditions in which more voices are heard now than a generation ago and some gatherings are multivoiced, but various restrictions remain and the church lurches from monovoiced to multivoiced practice and back again.

- Multivoiced church is desirable but challenging. This may be the hesitation of those who have caught the vision of multivoiced church and recognize how this might revolutionize their community but who know that moving toward this will not be easy and will likely meet resistance.

We want to encourage those who are drawn to multivoiced church to pursue this vision; to offer additional resources to those who already experience it; to warn those for whom it is familiar of the danger of slipping back into monovoiced ways unless practices are embedded and good habits developed; to provide a biblical and theological foundation for those who are uncertain about its legitimacy; and to share the experiences of others who are on the same journey.

Multivoiced church is, we believe, rooted in biblical teaching and practice, so in Chapter 2 we will give attention to the biblical foundations of this way of being church. Then we will trace, in Chapter 3, the checkered history of the church since the New Testament as it has oscillated between monovoiced and multivoiced expressions. We will sample a number of renewal movements that recovered multivoiced practices and consider the impact of the Christendom shift that nudged the church (at least in Europe) firmly in the monovoiced direction.

In Chapters 4 to 7 we will present a multivoiced approach to four vital features of church life: worship, learning, community building, and discernment. Our aim is to offer resources for those wanting to move in a multivoiced direction and guidance for those who want to sustain this approach. We believe that multivoiced church is natural for Christian communities but also that good habits and practices are needed if this is to be life-giving and fruitful.

Finally, in Chapter 8, we will return to the struggle to sustain multivoiced alternatives to the deep-seated monovoiced tradition. We will argue that this matters too much, not least if the church is to participate effectively in the mission of God, to allow the monovoiced tradition to hold sway; and we will encourage those who recognize the potential of multivoiced church to settle for nothing less.

We write as both practitioners and trainers. Both of us have been involved in local church leadership in decidedly multivoiced communities, and we are currently members of an inner-city church in Bristol, UK, with multivoiced features. We have explored various forms of multivoiced learning in many contexts over many years. Sian has wide experience of encouraging multivoiced worship; Stuart has modeled and encouraged multivoiced learning. And we have both been involved in training ministers in various traditions—some of whom have taken up the challenge of leading multivoiced churches and who have contributed to this book. We know of no church that practices all that we are writing about, but we know of many that embrace some features of multivoiced church.

We have encountered various reactions to our practice and teaching in this area. We have received enough positive feedback and enthusiasm to continue advocating multivoiced church, but not all have welcomed or appreciated our approach. Sometimes this seems to be little more than discomfort with what is unfamiliar (and slightly threatening), but some have raised serious concerns about what we are advocating. Won't this approach result in lower-quality teaching or pastoral care? Doesn't multivoiced learning mean the pooling of ignorance? What about the danger of heresy? What about authority in the church if all voices have to be heard? Isn't multivoiced church just too demanding?

We will try to address these and other concerns as we continue. But we will conclude this chapter by offering at least an initial answer to two basic questions.

What is multivoiced church?

Multivoiced church is an alternative to the dominant tradition in which large numbers of the Christian community are passive consumers instead of active participants. It replaces reliance on one person (variously designated as priest, vicar, minister, pastor, lead elder, or whatever) or a small group of people (elders, deacons, leadership team, church board, parochial church council, or whatever) with an expectation that the whole community is gifted, called, empowered, and expected to be involved in all aspects of church life.

This does not mean that all are equally gifted in all areas. Nor does it just apply to vocal participation, despite the term "multivoiced." Nor does it remove the need for leadership in the community—indeed, leadership is needed more than ever but it operates in a rather different way. Nor does it equate to a free-for-all, although it does mean a significant loss of institutional control, which many find threatening.

In relation to *worship* it means equipping many voices to express praise to God in many ways, to share their own stories as they retell the big story of God, and to express the full range of human emotions as they pour out their hearts to God in prayer. This does not abolish the role of "worship leaders," but it dramatically reduces our dependence on them.

In relation to *learning* it means being more concerned about what is learned and put into practice than presentational skills, giving attention to diverse learning styles, exploring alternatives to monologue sermons, and developing learning communities that know how to wrestle with the biblical text and apply it to their lives. This does not abolish preaching, but it dramatically reduces our dependence on preachers.

In relation to *community* it means nurturing authentic friendships that go well beyond superficial or institutional ways of relating, embracing mutual accountability and mutual support, developing agreed-upon processes for dealing with disagreements, and moving beyond a firefighting pastoral care strategy to build disciple-making communities. This does not abolish pastors or pastoral teams, but it dramatically reduces our dependence on them.

In relation to *discernment* it means believing that the community can seek the mind of Christ together, confident in the direction of the Spirit and hopeful of reaching a united decision. It means drawing out the reticent, including the marginalized, listening for the prophetic minority, and developing processes to ensure all are heard and that decisions are made without undue delay. This does not abolish vision casting and decisive action, but it dramatically increases the community's ownership of what is decided.

We are contrasting monovoiced and multivoiced expressions of church quite starkly. In reality, many churches exhibit features of both, although often monovoiced features are dominant in some areas of church life even if other areas are more multivoiced. But the power of the monovoiced tradition is so strong that multivoiced practices can easily default back to monovoiced patterns. Our concern in this book is to offer resources and advocate habits that will help churches introduce and sustain multivoiced practices.

Why does multivoiced church matter?

But how important is it for churches to be multivoiced? Among the multiple challenges we face, especially in the context of post-Christendom Western societies, where does this apparently internal issue rank? Evidently, our assumption is that it is worth devoting the time needed to write a book on the subject. But are there not more pressing, and more missional, concerns?

Our changing culture is certainly one of the reasons why we believe churches need to be more multivoiced than they have often been. We are not arguing that churches should be conformed to or co-opted by cultural preferences, but neither can they exist in isolation from their surroundings. As we reflect on our culture, especially in times of transition, we may find this helps us identify which of our convictions and practices are truly biblical and authentically Christian, and which have been influenced by or are even captive to a previous culture.

The dominance of the monologue sermon, as we will see, is a classic example of this. It is not just that we question the place of preaching because postmodern culture reacts badly to unchallengable monologues (though it does), but that *this* culture shift prompts us to ask questions about how a *previous* culture shift influenced the primacy the church gave to preaching in an earlier era, driving us back to the New Testament to examine the role preaching played in the early churches.

Post-Christendom represents a much more serious challenge to the churches in Western societies than post-modernity, although this also opens up many fresh opportunities. For the foreseeable future churches are going to have fewer resources, and most will be unable to sustain the level of activities that could be sustained in the Christendom era. Church life will need to be simplified and church members will need to take more responsibility for the life and mission of their community. Many churches will be unable to afford full-time staff, and bivocational ministry will become increasingly common. Multivoiced church will no longer be a luxury but a necessity if churches are to thrive or even survive.

> In England, around four hundred village shops are closing each year, unable to compete with out-of-town supermarkets or to sustain full-time paid shopkeepers. Where these shops (which are often at the heart of the local community) survive it is because the villagers take the initiative, raise money to buy and stock them, offer their time as voluntary shopkeepers, and encourage their neighbors to shop locally. They are no longer passive consumers but active participants—an encouraging analogy.

In post-Christendom there will be fewer cultural supports for faith, many more lifestyle options and numerous disincentives to discipleship. Passive attendance at weekly front-led worship events, however inspiring, and passive consumption of sermons, however well crafted, will not do. Monovoiced churches have a tendency to foster dependency rather than maturity, to validate individualism rather than encouraging mutuality. But we will need one another if we are to live faithfully and counterculturally in an increasingly alien culture. We will need churches that can function as communities of discernment and resistance, churches that can hold us accountable and support us in making surprising lifestyle choices, churches that are multivoiced enough to help us wrestle with issues and work though struggles.

Multivoiced church matters because this is our best hope of reversing the alarming trend toward biblical and theological illiteracy, reducing chronic dependency, rescuing church leaders from self-absorption and toxic levels of stress, becoming authentic disciples and helping others on the journey, and creating and sustaining healthy communities. Multivoiced church matters because it is the biblical pattern, however much cultural influences and prevailing church practices have obscured this over the centuries.

And multivoiced church matters for the sake of mission. Active participants in healthy multivoiced churches are much more likely to be confident in sharing their faith, ready to engage in social action, hospitable to their neighbors, alert to pastoral opportunities beyond the church, and able to participate in dialogue and debate. There is one proviso, which we need to bear in mind throughout this book and to which we will return: multivoiced must not mean busy! Healthy multivoiced churches share responsibilities in such a way that time and energy are released rather than consumed in internal maintenance.

There is a tendency in some circles to oppose "incarnational" and "attractional" models of mission, advocating the former over the latter. This has been a necessary corrective in a context where churches have long prioritized "come" over "go." But authentic mission is both "go and tell" and "come and see." However radical and creative our incarnational mission strategies are, they need the authentication of healthy and attractive Christian communities. Our contention is that such communities emerge in multivoiced churches.

2

Biblical Foundations of Multivoiced Church

Pentecost and prophecy

If multivoiced church tends to reemerge in periods of spiritual renewal, we should not be surprised that this expression of Christian community permeates Luke's account of the Day of Pentecost.[1] Nor should we miss the powerful connection in this passage between multivoiced church and mission.

When the Holy Spirit fell on the disciples gathered in an upper room in Jerusalem, Luke reports that they all began to praise God, using various languages that were recognized by the crowd that came to find out what all the noise was about so early in the morning. The impact of this multivoiced and multilingual community was profound. Although some sneered, many stayed to listen as Peter interpreted what was happening and invited them to join this bewildering but attractive community. And over three thousand decided to do so.

---

1. Acts 2.

What happened on the Day of Pentecost has often been understood as a reversal of what occurred at the Tower of Babel.[2] When the Lord confused their languages the people were scattered because they could no longer understand each other. Now, many centuries later, people from many language groups gather because they can understand what the disciples are saying. What would otherwise have been an alienating cacophony is transformed by God's Spirit into a winsome experience of multivoiced worship.

Actually, exhilarating and portentous as the Day of Pentecost is, it points forward to the ultimate reversal of Babel when people from every tribe, people, and language worship together in multivoiced harmony around the throne of God.[3] What is striking, though, about both accounts is that the antidote to confusion and cacophony is not uniformity or control but Spirit-inspired harmonious diversity. We will encounter this antidote again in the writings of Paul.

But back to the Day of Pentecost. The worship may be multivoiced, but the preaching is monovoiced as Peter stands up and seizes the opportunity to proclaim the gospel. There is a time and place for monovoiced proclamation. Multivoiced church does not preclude this or minimize its significance. Sometimes what is needed is a clear, authoritative word from a single spokesperson. But this need not be the dominant or default mode of church life and ministry.

And it is interesting to note that, although Peter spoke, he stood up "with the eleven" and, when he had finished speaking, the crowd responded not only to him but also "to the other apostles," asking all of them what they should do. So this most iconic of monologue sermons is, in fact, set in the context of a band of brothers standing together, representing the embryonic church community.[4]

The content of Peter's speech is also highly significant for our discussion. Before calling the crowd to think again about the

---

2. Gen 11:1-9.

3. Rev 7:9-10.

4. We are aware that Peter is viewed by some, especially on the basis of Matt 16:18, as having a foundational role in the church that sets him and his successors apart from others. This interpretation, which has enhanced the tendency to monovoiced church practices, we find unconvincing.

significance of recent events in Jerusalem, he quotes from the prophet Joel:

> ✗ [In the last days, God says,]
> I will pour out my Spirit on all people.
> Your sons and daughters will prophesy,
>   your old men will dream dreams,
>   your young men will see visions,
> Even on my servants, both men and women,
>   I will pour out my Spirit in those days.[5]

What the crowd had witnessed that morning was startlingly new but not unanticipated. A persistent expectation within the prophetic tradition of Israel was that one day the Spirit would be poured out much more liberally than under the old covenant. No longer would the Spirit's anointing be primarily associated with kings, priests, and prophets. Instead, all of God's people would receive the Spirit and participate in a multivoiced community.

A well-known incident from early in Israel's history sets the scene.[6] Discouraged by the constant grumbling of the Israelites in the wilderness, Moses bemoans the burden he is carrying alone. The Lord's response is to endue seventy elders with some of "the Spirit that was on him" so that they could share Moses's burden. When the Spirit rested on them, they prophesied—one overburdened prophet had been joined by seventy others. Weary preachers and pastors in many churches today might yearn for such shared ministry.

But the story continues. Two of the elders designated for this experience had not turned up at the tent of meeting but were found prophesying in the camp. Concerned about this apparently unauthorized activity and the threat to Moses's authority, young Joshua informs Moses and urges him to stop them. Moses understands his assistant's concern but replies, "I wish that all the LORD's people were prophets and that the LORD would put his Spirit on them!" Multivoiced church is possible when church leaders are as unthreatened as Moses by evidence that God is able to speak through many people.

---

5. Joel 2:28-29.
6. Num 11:1-30.

The prophets picked up this vision of a Spirit-endued community and associated it with a new covenant that was coming. Jeremiah writes:

> "This is the covenant I will make with the house of Israel
>   after that time," declares the LORD.
> "I will put my law in their minds
>   and write it on their hearts.
> I will be their God,
>   and they will be my people.
> No longer will they teach their neighbors,
>   or say to one another, 'Know the LORD,'
> because they will all know me,
> from the least of them to the greatest,"
>   declares the LORD.[7]

Peter could have referred to the incident in Numbers or quoted this familiar passage from Jeremiah. But he turns to the prophet Joel, who links the outpouring of the Spirit with the "last days," the time when the purposes of God reach their climax. As so often in the New Testament, the "last days" seem to have a double focus—some of what Joel predicts finds fulfillment on the Day of Pentecost as the Spirit descends, but some awaits the end of the age. And Joel's punch line—"And everyone who calls on the name of the Lord will be saved"[8]—is ideal for Peter's context. "Save yourselves from this corrupt generation," he pleads with the crowd.

Joel's vision of a Spirit-empowered and multivoiced community is comprehensive. Men and women, young and old—all are equipped by the Spirit to dream dreams, see visions, and prophesy. Peter declares that this vision is becoming a reality and urges the crowd to repent so that they too can receive, not only forgiveness of their sins, but the gift of the Holy Spirit. This gift, he promises, is available to "all whom the Lord our God will call."

---

7. Jer 31:33-34.
8. Acts 2:21, quoting Joel 2:32.

The biblical foundation for multivoiced church is here on the Day of Pentecost, deeply rooted in the prophetic tradition and worked out in the experience of the early churches.

Domesticity and dialogue

Those who responded positively to Peter's message joined an exuberant community that spent a lot of time together, meeting either in their homes or in the temple courts. Luke gives us a thumbnail sketch of this community, which was characterized by hospitality and shared meals, prayer and worship, signs and wonders, learning from the apostles, fellowship, and generous sharing of possessions. Already quite sizable, the community was growing daily.[9] Many aspects of this picture, sometimes dismissed as an idealized portrait, are familiar from periods of revival and renewal in the history of the church.

Much of the activity, throughout Acts and for many decades later, took place in homes. Meetings in the temple courts in Jerusalem,[10] larger gatherings in Solomon's Colonnade,[11] and visits to synagogues in various places reflect the efforts of the community to continue to interact with their fellow Jews (until the level of opposition made this too difficult), but the churches nourished their community life and developed their distinctive practices in domestic settings.

Where a community meets impacts the way its members interact and the practices they adopt, as does the size of the community. Architecture, furniture, seating arrangements, acoustics, décor, and ethos are all very influential. Communities that meet in buildings set out as a lecture hall or a performance space tend to become passive spectators of action at the front of the building. Communities seated behind each other in fixed seats struggle to escape individualized expressions of worship. Massive congregations make multivoiced participation more difficult. We will return to this issue when we investigate the influence of specialized church buildings on the practice of multivoiced church.

---

9. Acts 2:42-47.
10. Acts 2:46; 3:1.
11. Acts 5:12.

But the early churches met mainly in homes and in relatively small communities. They broke bread and shared wine in the context of domestic meals. They devoted themselves to the apostles' teaching in domestic spaces. They prayed and worshiped in settings where they also chatted, laughed, played, and worked. Not only did this offer protection against the persistent tendency of religions to become dualistic, separating sacred activities and places from secular, but it inevitably and profoundly shaped the kind of communities that emerged.

Several years ago Stuart was teaching at a weekend conference organized by a Baptist church, which took place at Ashburnham Place, a conference center in Sussex, UK. He was struggling to persuade an apparently rather passive group to engage with him and with one another. He suggested moving the next session out of the large room which was set up in lecture mode and into the courtyard, where people could sit around small café tables. The change of location and seating arrangements made an immediate difference. In the next two sessions conversations were taking place all over the courtyard and the community was energized and naturally interactive.

Multivoiced church is inherently more likely to develop and be sustained in domestic settings, whether or not this is intentional, and whether or not the practice is undergirded by principles that have been carefully thought out. Dialogue is so much more natural than monologue in domestic settings, in small groups, and in contexts where people are able to eyeball one another. It is perfectly possible for one person to speak for a while, even quite a long while,[12] but it would be strange in a domestic setting if this were not followed by discussion, questions, and comments. And very often in this context interruptions will be allowed or encouraged. Group dynamics tend to ensure that dialogue occurs.

---

12. An unusual example, with disturbing consequences but a happy ending, can be found in Acts 20:7-12.

Similarly, in a domestic setting it is much less likely that spoken prayers, Bible readings, expressions of praise, or other forms of worship are voiced exclusively by one person. It is inevitable that some members of the community will be more vocal than others, but this is very different from the widespread silence and passivity in monovoiced churches. The emphasis is on participation rather than performance.

These dynamics are very familiar in churches that have introduced home groups, house groups, cell groups, or whatever terminology is used for smaller, usually midweek, groups that encourage the kind of interaction and dialogue that is not typical of larger gatherings, usually on Sundays. Many churches do have experience of multivoiced community, but in most this is subsidiary, dispensable, and unsupported by training in how to participate. Furthermore, such churches can all too easily assume that this is sufficient and so fail to engage with the challenge of being multivoiced in many other dimensions of church life, including what happens on Sundays (or whenever the whole community gathers).

But for the churches we encounter in the New Testament, domesticity and multivoiced community were normal, rather than exceptional or secondary. And this affected not only the ways in which they learned and worshiped but also their approach to leadership, pastoral care, decision making, and economics. Having summarized the features of the emerging church in Jerusalem, Luke continues to paint a picture of a multivoiced community, not only in Jerusalem but in the diverse contexts in which churches began to appear. It seems that, even in larger gatherings, multivoiced practices persisted. Here is a sample of the evidence:

- The believers "raised their voices together in prayer to God" (Acts 4:24).

- They shared their possessions with others, exhibiting the kind of pastoral care that requires deep friendship and openness about financial needs (Acts 4:32-35).

- They resolved difficulties through consultation and shared decision making (Acts 6:1-6).

• They engaged in theological reflection together on the cultural and ethical issues involved in pioneering mission initiatives (Acts 11:1-18).

• The church at Antioch was led by a team of prophets and teachers and discerned the call of God as they worshiped together (Acts 13:1-3).

• Paul and Barnabas appointed elders in each church they planted, establishing plural leadership as normal (Acts 14:23).

• The Jerusalem church debated contentious issues as a whole community, hearing different perspectives, but reached agreement and communicated with churches in other places as a "whole church" (Acts 15:22).

During recent decades there has been a global explosion of churches meeting primarily in domestic settings. Known variously as cell churches, base ecclesial communities, house churches, table churches, household churches, or simple churches, these have proliferated in many different cultures. This development can be explained and interpreted in several ways, and it will be some time yet before its sustainability and missional potential can be properly assessed, but in these communities multivoiced church is natural and normal. It will be interesting to see whether this continues as the communities mature and whether multivoiced practices also characterize the larger gatherings they organize.

Using the book of Acts to establish a biblical foundation for the practice of multivoiced church may raise some exegetical eyebrows. After all, Luke's account is punctuated with set-piece monologues: Peter in Jerusalem and in the house of Cornelius; Stephen before his accusers; Paul in many cities in Asia Minor and Europe and on trial before various authorities. But multivoiced church need not preclude monologue in contexts where this is the most appropriate mode of communication. And careful analysis of Luke's account reveals a surprising number of dialogical terms alongside the speeches—arguing, asking, proving, conversing, debating, explaining, persuading, discussing, refuting, convincing.[13] Luke quite often uses *dialegomai*, the word from which our term "dialogue" is derived, to describe Paul's approach. He also commends the Jewish community in Berea because, when they heard Paul's message, they "examined the Scriptures every day to see if what Paul said was true."[14] Active engagement is preferable to passive reception, it seems.

Participation and plurality

The Epistles fill out our understanding of how the early churches operated and the values and principles that undergirded their practices, although we learn surprisingly little about their structure and inner dynamics. As we read the various letters we need to bear in mind that they were written to individuals or small communities that met in homes and avoid the temptation to interpret them as if they were addressed to large congregations meeting in dedicated buildings.

The most extended discussion of what happened when the early Christians met together appears in 1 Corinthians 11-14. Although Paul's instructions here are directed toward a particular church, and practices in other churches may have been different, he does refer to the customs of other churches to support the counsel he is offering, so it is likely that the same principles were operative, even if there were cultural variations.[15]

The church in Corinth was markedly multivoiced! So much so, in fact, that the meetings were chaotic and unedifying. Disorder, indiscipline, misuse of spiritual gifts, lack of care for one another,

---

13. For example, Acts 6:9; 8:30; 9:22, 29; 10:29; 13:43; 15:2; 17:2-3, 17-20; 18:19, 28; 19:8-9, 26; 20:7, 11; 28:23. Paul Warby has identified sixty-eight preaching/teaching events in Acts, twenty-eight of which give no information about whether these are monologues or dialogues. Of the remaining forty, there is dialogue in thirty-three cases and in another fourteen someone other than the main speaker initiates the event. Only five are clearly monologues. See www.anabaptistnetwork.com/node/423.
14. Acts 17:11.
15. 1 Cor 11:16; 14:33, 36.

failure to share their resources, and lack of concern for the witness of the church to outsiders were all damaging the community, however exciting it all seemed. If there was a case for restricting multivoiced church and reasserting monovoiced church, surely Corinth demonstrates this. But Paul's response is wholeheartedly to endorse multivoiced church and to give detailed advice about how this can become more effective.[16]

The best way to appreciate the multivoiced nature of the church at Corinth and the way that Paul encourages the community to develop this is to read through this long passage. We know that readers of books like this are often reluctant to heed the encouragement to open their Bibles and study the text for themselves, but we cannot do justice here to the many different aspects of multivoiced church that are evident in these chapters.[17] All we can offer is a summary of some of the most pertinent points:

- Eating the Lord's Supper involves more than individual participation—sharing resources, "discerning the body" (NRSV), practicing hospitality, and honoring each other are essential components (11:20-34).

- Each member of the community is gifted by the Spirit to contribute something that will be "for the common good" (12:7; 14:26).

- The church community is patterned on the human body, which "does not consist of one member but of many" (12:14 NRSV).

- All the gifts are needed, so multivoiced church is essential, and special concern must be exercised to ensure weaker members can play their part (12:20-2).

---

16. For an extended discussion of this passage, see Alan Kreider and Eleanor Kreider, *Worship and Mission After Christendom* (Harrisonburg: Herald Press, 2011), 94–109.

17. For a detailed discussion of these chapters, see Kreider and Kreider, *Worship and Mission After Christendom.*

- Participating sensitively in multivoiced church is an expression of love for the community (13:1-3; 14:1).

- The goal of multivoiced church is to build up, encourage, and console the whole community, so participation must be honed to enable this to happen (14:3, 5, 12, 26, 31).

- Multivoiced church functions effectively if it is well-ordered and peaceful, and if each contribution is weighed carefully (14:33, 40).

- For multivoiced communities to develop and mature there must be opportunities for learning and growth to take place (14:31).

- When multivoiced church is working well, it has missional potency: the impact on outsiders is profound (14:24-25).

From other New Testament letters we pick up indications that multivoiced church was not limited to Corinth. Romans 12:4-8 and 1 Peter 4:10-11 encourage members of the community to be active and vocal, using whatever gifts they have received from God. Galatians 6:1-2, James 5:19, and 1 John 5:16 place the responsibility for helping those who fall into sin on all members of the community, not just on those who lead the church. Ephesians 4:7-16 employs soaring language to envision the church reaching maturity only when every member of the body is fully functioning and making its distinctive contribution. Colossians 3:16 encourages the church to recognize the responsibility and capacity of its members to teach and admonish one another. First Thessalonians 5:12-22 recognizes the role of leaders in the community but urges all the brothers and sisters to be involved in pastoral care, admonishing, exercising spiritual gifts, and testing these various contributions. Hebrews 10:24-5 identifies as the main reasons for continuing to meet together "provoking one another to love and good deeds . . . encouraging one another"(NRSV). And throughout the Epistles, whatever terms are used, we encounter plural leadership in the churches and diversity of gifts in the leadership teams.

What did Jesus do and say?

Throughout the centuries, renewal and restorationist movements have delved into the New Testament in order to discern the essential features of the earliest churches. This has been an exhilarating but unending search, as subsequent movements have rejected or refined the conclusions of previous movements and laid claim to a further recovery of authentic New Testament practices. As we have noted already, many of the movements stumbled afresh on the multivoiced practices of the early Christians. But too often this search has been restricted to Acts and the Epistles, perhaps assuming that the Gospels have little to offer on this subject. After all, the word *church* only appears in two passages in the Gospel of Matthew and not at all in the other Gospels.

But the Gospels were written for the benefit of churches that were multiplying, reflecting theologically on diverse cultural, ethical, and pastoral issues, engaging in mission among Jews and Gentiles, and working out how to embody in their community life the values Jesus had taught and modeled. They may not use the term *church* often, but they offer rich resources on the shape of church life. And they point us back beyond the churches to Jesus as the source of their inspiration. The most radical renewal movements have always taken their lead from Jesus rather than the early churches.

When we examine the Gospels and ask what Jesus did and said that might be relevant to our exploration of multivoiced church, we may be surprised by what we discover. If we start with the two references to "church," the first—"I will build my church, and the gates of Hades will not prevail against it" (Matt 16:18 nrsv)—is encouraging but does not seem to offer any guidelines about the nature of this community. The second, however, is very significant for our purposes. Here (Matt 18:15-20) Jesus spells out a process for his disciples to work through when there is sin in the community and the threat of division.

What is striking about this is that the only *explicit* instruction about church life reported from the teaching of Jesus envisages a multivoiced community that exercises pastoral care when brothers or sisters are struggling with sin or hurting one another. Of course, much of what Jesus teaches and models has implicit relevance for church life (and often seems to require a multivoiced community), but his only explicit instruction has nothing to say about leadership, membership, preaching, worship, organization, the sacraments, or most of the issues to which churches give so much attention.

Instead, Jesus encourages his disciples, when necessary, to confront one another in order to maintain the integrity of the community and to "regain" (18:15 NRSV) struggling brothers and sisters. It is in this context that we find the well-known assurance that "where two or three are gathered in my name, I am there among them" (18:20 NRSV)—a further reminder that small domestic settings are the primary context for the teaching of the New Testament. In these intimate settings, but often not in larger institutional contexts, the process Jesus spells out can be meaningful, restorative, and community enhancing.[18]

Another surprise awaiting unsuspecting Gospel researchers is that Jesus rarely preaches a sermon. This can come as a shock to those who belong to churches in which monologue sermons are very frequent and appear to be the preeminent mode of communication. But the Gospels contain very few monologue sermons. The major exceptions are the Sermon on the Mount (Matthew 5–7; the abbreviated version in Luke 6:20-49 is often referred to as the Sermon on the Plain) and a number of passages in John's Gospel. Elsewhere Jesus devises parables, tells stories, asks questions (but rarely answers them), teaches through symbolic actions, engages people in conversation, invites others to interpret Scripture, and presents those who listen to him with enigmatic sayings that require them to wrestle with their meaning.[19]

---

18. We will explore this process further in Chapter 6.
19. Paul Warby concludes that in Mark's Gospel only ten out of the sixty-three teaching events recorded in Jesus' ministry are clearly

And yet Jesus declared at the beginning of his public ministry that the Spirit of the Lord had anointed him for a ministry of proclamation.[20] Matthew's Gospel, in particular, is at pains to present Jesus as the Teacher, and people frequently address Jesus in this way. His disciples, and even his opponents, acknowledged that he taught with authority and much that he said and did was recognizably within the prophetic preaching tradition. But Jesus' ministry seems not to have required the unremitting use of monologues (any more than contemporary rabbis would have relied on such monochrome teaching methods).

If Jesus is our model and teacher, not only in what he said but in how he said it, we may need to reconsider the dominant role of monologue sermons in many churches. There is a place for proclamation and for authoritative teaching if we follow the example of Jesus, but there is no justification in the Gospels for exalting this mode of communication over all others. Jesus much more often models dialogue and multivoiced community, inviting others to participate actively in the learning process. Renewal movements that have been inspired by fresh encounters with the Gospels have sometimes recognized this and have explored alternative ways of learning together.

The purpose of this chapter has been to demonstrate that multivoiced church is built on solid biblical foundations. The Old Testament, and in particular the prophetic tradition, anticipates this kind of community as a consequence of the outpouring of the Spirit. The New Testament offers numerous examples of multivoiced church in action and provides crucial correctives to ensure that multivoiced practices are healthy. The Gospels indicate that multivoiced church is rooted firmly in the teaching and practice of Jesus. Revelation (to which we have referred only in passing) confirms that our eternal destiny is to become participants in a multivoiced choir of worshipers and citizens of a multijeweled

---

monologues—and even in those cases there are elements of dialogue associated with some of them. See www.anabaptistnetwork.com/node/423. Others have reached similar conclusions.

20. Luke 4:18.

city into which the multicultural treasures of all nations will be brought to honor God.

In light of all this, it is not surprising that renewal movements have frequently recovered the practices of multivoiced church. What is surprising is how powerfully entrenched the monovoiced church tradition is and how easily multivoiced church defaults to this. For an explanation, we turn next to the story of the church beyond the New Testament and the influences brought to bear upon it as it grew and spread.

3

The Rise and Fall of Multivoiced Church

From multivoiced to monovoiced

The mandate ringing in the ears of the disciples as Jesus left them, according to Luke at the beginning of Acts, was to be witnesses to all that had happened "in Jerusalem, and in all Judea and Samaria, and to the ends of the earth."[1] Luke ends his narrative with Paul in Rome—at the center of the Western world—but still hoping to travel on to distant lands.[2] He has focused on the western advance of the gospel, rather than on those who went east, and especially on Paul's travels and exploits. But throughout Acts there are indications of the many people who were involved in this multivoiced missionary movement.

Paul was not a lone heroic missionary but the leader of a series of missionary bands, with team members joining and leaving, remaining behind or going on ahead, numbering over thirty in total. Nor was he the only missionary or team leader. Nor was

---

1. Acts 1:8.
2. Acts 28:16-31; cf. Rom 15:23-4.

all the missionary activity organized, authorized, and recorded. Unnamed missionaries proclaimed the gospel and planted churches in many places, including Rome itself, before Paul arrived. Indeed, it seems that the recognized leaders of the church (those designated as apostles—"sent ones") were sometimes the most reluctant to seize opportunities to carry the good news to new places.[3] Often they appear to be playing catch-up.[4]

By the end of the first century, then, through the efforts of this multivoiced missionary movement, Christian communities had been established in many of the major cities of the eastern Roman Empire and in the capital city. As in the New Testament, they gathered in homes and wherever they might escape detection in an environment that was suspicious of this new sect and often hostile. And as in the New Testament, this domestic setting and the small size of these communities would have meant that multivoiced church remained normal.

But would this pattern of community life persist as the church grew and spread? Over the next two centuries, churches were planted in more and more communities—in the west of the empire as well as the east, and in small towns and villages as well as the cities. By the beginning of the fourth century, historians estimate that as many as six million people (a tenth of the empire) might have been Christians. The church was still on the margins of society, still subject to accusations, scapegoating, and worse—including the empire-wide persecution initiated by Diocletian at the very end of the third century—but it was now a sizable community with some larger congregations, a well-developed organizational and leadership structure, and some buildings designated specifically for church activities. Had it retained any of its multivoiced practices, or had these disappeared as they would do in the later generations of many subsequent movements?

The evidence suggests that institutionalization and clericalization were taking their toll, but that multivoiced church life was

---

3. Acts 8:1.
4. For example, Acts 8:14; 11:22.

still the experience of many communities—and that the first major protest movement in church history was galvanized, at least in part, by the demise of multivoiced practices.

Three witnesses to the persistence of multivoiced church life (and to institutionalism on the rise) are Tertullian, Clement of Alexandria, and the document known as the *Apostolic Constitutions*.

Tertullian (*ca.* 160–*ca.* 220)

Tertullian lived in Carthage, in North Africa. He was the first church leader to write extensively in Latin and the first we know of to have used the term *Trinity* (he is sometimes known as the "father of Latin Christianity"). His writings are theological and apologetic—explaining and defending Christian teaching—but he is concerned also with the life and health of the church. And in his writings we read of congregations that were decidedly multivoiced.

In his *Apology*, Tertullian describes what happens when the church meets together. He is concerned not only to defend the Christian community against unwarranted accusations but also to commend its practices. "We meet together as an assembly and congregation," he writes, "that, offering up prayer to God as with united force, we may wrestle with Him in our supplications."[5] "We assemble to read our sacred writings," he continues. "With the sacred words we nourish our faith, we animate our hope, we make our confidence more steadfast; and no less by inculcations of God's precepts we confirm good habits. In the same place also exhortations are made, rebukes and sacred censures are administered."

It is possible, of course, to interpret this passage in a monovoiced way, with designated leaders of the congregation doing all the praying, reading, exhorting, and rebuking, and it is clear that the congregation had leaders. Tertullian writes: "The tried men of our elders preside over us, obtaining that honor not by

---

5. All quotations are from Tertullian's *Apology* 39. We are grateful to Alan Kreider for drawing our attention to this and other relevant passages in early church documents.

purchase, but by established character." But there is much else in this passage that points in a multivoiced direction.

Tertullian next explains the economic sharing that characterizes the Christian community. In a classic passage that indicates how far away the early churches were from the tithing mentality that would characterize the medieval churches (and some churches today), he acknowledges "we have our treasure-chest" but insists this is "not made up of purchase-money." The churches do not demand fees from members, nor are the gifts gathered used to support professional clergy. Instead, he describes a relaxed approach: "If he likes, each puts in a small donation; but only if it be his pleasure, and only if he be able: for there is no compulsion; all is voluntary. These gifts are, as it were, piety's deposit fund." And the donations are recycled within the community: "to support and bury poor people, to supply the wants of boys and girls destitute of means and parents, and of old persons confined now to the house; such, too, as have suffered shipwreck; and if there happen to be any in the mines, or banished to the islands, or shut up in the prisons, for nothing but their fidelity to the cause of God's Church."

The context for the praying, reading of Scripture, exhorting and rebuking, and gathering and disbursing of resources is the *agape* or "love feast." This celebration meal prompted many of the accusations leveled against the early churches. Tertullian complains that the pagans "abuse also our humble feasts, on the ground that they are extravagant as well as infamously wicked." They are not orgies, he insists, but "modest" meals that are shared in an atmosphere of reverence and prayerfulness. "As much is eaten as satisfies the cravings of hunger; as much is drunk as befits the chaste," he reports. And he offers as "a proof of the measure of our drinking" a regular multivoiced practice: "each is asked to stand forth and sing, as he can, a hymn to God, either one from the holy Scriptures or one of his own composing." We could not do this, he implies, if we were all drunk!

The "love feast" that Tertullian describes would later be outlawed by a church determined to clamp down on unregulated, multivoiced church life. Celebration of the eucharist in a mono-voiced and clerical church must be detached from a real meal at which there might be (surely would be) conversation and partici-pation rather than quiet observation of holy mysteries performed by authorized church leaders. But, in the churches Tertullian knew, the "love feast" was at the heart of a multivoiced commu-nity that shared their resources, songs, prayers, reflections, and exhortations.

Clement of Alexandria (ca. 150–ca. 215)

Clement of Alexandria, a contemporary of Tertullian, was a phi-losopher and church leader in Alexandria, in Egypt, one of the leading centers of early Christianity. He was a theologian writ-ing in Greek and head of a famous catechetical school (for teach-ing new believers). In one of the chapters of his *Paedagogus* ("The Instructor"), he addresses the issue that concerned Tertullian—the accusation that church meetings were riotous and immoral banquets.[6]

Clement spends most of this chapter describing and critiquing pagan festivals, rather than explaining what happens when the church meets, but the fact that these criticisms are so common and that church leaders needed to defend their gatherings against such charges offers compelling evidence that they were partici-patory and multivoiced, not occasions where most were passive spectators. Christians in Alexandria, as in Carthage, met around meal tables and interwove their praying and worshiping with eat-ing and conversation.

Clement, "distinguishing from such revelry the divine service," points to the inspiration of the Spirit, who prompts church mem-bers to use their tongues like musical instruments. In a rather con-voluted passage with extensive use of imagery he claims that "the tongue is the psaltery of the Lord" and refers to "the mouth struck by the Spirit, as it were by a plectrum." Quoting from Colossians—"teaching and admonishing one another in all wisdom, in psalms, and hymns, and spiritual songs, singing with grace in your heart

---

6. All quotations are from Clement of Alexandria, *Paedagogus* 2.4.

to God"—he concludes: "this is our thankful revelry." Clement goes on to describe the meal shared by the Christian community, preceded and followed by prayers of thanksgiving. His point throughout this chapter is that church meetings may have formal similarities with pagan banquets, but their atmosphere, purpose, and conduct is quite different.

Was it necessary for the church later to restrict such multi-voiced gatherings that fused worship with eating together? Had these persistent pagan accusations taken their toll? Or was this rather an increasingly institutionalized church exercising control and silencing the many voices that would naturally be raised in such contexts? Whatever the reason, it is clear from Clement's writings that in earlier days such gatherings were normal and that they need not be undisciplined or unseemly.

> When Stuart was involved in church planting in East London in the 1980s, the emerging Christian community had no building of its own but met either in homes or, as it grew larger, in hired premises. The church ate together each Sunday and there was always animated conversation and often plenty of laughter. But it came as a surprise when the church was told it could no longer use a particular building because of the "wild parties" it was holding. Despite being convinced this accusation was actually leveled at another group using the building, the church could not persuade the owners to relent. Stuart rather enjoys having been involved in a church accused of the same shameful behavior as the early Christians!

The *Apostolic Constitutions*

The *Apostolic Constitutions* is a collection of eight treatises, written probably between 375 and 380 by an unknown author, and usually associated with the church in Antioch (another of the leading centers of early Christianity and an avowed rival of Alexandria). Though purporting to reflect the teaching and practice of the first apostles, this document inevitably reflects the assumptions and practices of its own time. It offers guidance on a range of issues relating to doctrine, worship, and church order.

Two centuries later than Clement or Tertullian, it indicates that even when the church of the margins was moving toward the imperial center there was still residual evidence of multivoiced practices. Originating in a different region of the empire, it suggests that in Syria, as in Egypt and Carthage, some features of multivoiced church life persisted for generations beyond the New Testament.

But the multivoiced practices here do seem residual, and the atmosphere of the church gatherings described in these treatises is much less convivial and much more formal. In the second treatise[7] instructions are given to the presiding bishop, spelling out in great detail matters of order and good conduct. Attention is given to the seating arrangements, the position of items of furniture, and the order in which various elements of the service are to take place. Roles and titles are carefully distinguished—bishop, presbyter, deacon, deaconess, catechumen, penitent—and the places assigned to men and women, children, and older people are clearly identified. This is an ordered community and a controlled environment.

The treatise employs the imagery of a great ship, with the bishop as its commander. He is instructed, when calling the church together: "appoint the assemblies to be made with all possible skill, charging the deacons as mariners to prepare places for the brethren as for passengers, with all due care and decency." Designating the congregation as "passengers" is an ominous development, as is the instruction: "let the laity sit on the other side, with all quietness and good order." The separation between active, vocal clergy and passive, silent laity indicates that we are now in a different era from Tertullian's and Clement's.[8]

---

7. All quotations are from *Apostolic Constitutions* 2.57.

8. We are using the terms *clergy* and *laity* here and elsewhere in this book in the way they are commonly used—but this does not mean that we endorse this usage.

And yet there are still many voices in this assembly and, apparently, some freedom as to which voices will be heard: ". . . when there have been two lessons severally read, let some other person sing the hymns of David, and let the people join at the conclusions of the verses . . . and afterward let a deacon or a presbyter read the Gospels." The concern for good order is evident—". . . while the Gospel is read, let all the presbyters and deacons, and all the people, stand up in great silence"—but provision is also made for several people to preach after the Scripture is read: "In the next place, let the presbyters one by one, not all together, exhort the people, and the bishop in the last place."

This concern for good order and reverence is apparent in a later passage: ". . . let the deacon oversee the people, that nobody may whisper, nor slumber, nor laugh, nor nod; for all ought in the church to stand wisely, and soberly, and attentively, having their attention fixed upon the word of the Lord." By the end of the fourth century, at least, there seem to have been some attending who were less than wholeheartedly involved in the service—but perhaps this is inevitable as participation moves toward passivity. But once again this is immediately followed by an expectation that many will participate in the prayers: "After this, let all rise up with one consent, and looking toward the east . . . pray to God." And as the service moves toward its eucharistic climax, all are invited to share the kiss of peace before some of the clergy attend to the bread and wine while others are warned to "watch the multitude, and keep them silent."

What we seem to have in the *Apostolic Constitutions* is evidence of significant transition from an earlier multivoiced and domestic form of church to a more institutional, clerical, and ordered gathering. Worship has been detached from sharing a meal together (by now most churches met in the morning, when time was necessarily limited, rather than in the evening, when there was more time to relax together, which no doubt further restricted multivoiced church). There are vestiges of past practice in the number of voices that can still be heard, but their roles are circumscribed, and repeated instructions anticipate the silencing of the laity that will become normative in the coming years.

Montanism—a multivoiced protest movement

The earliest renewal movement in the history of the church emerged around 170 in Asia Minor—and like many later movements the recovery of multivoiced church was one of its distinctive features. Although more commonly known by historians as "Montanism," after one of its leaders, Montanus, the movement was known to its contemporaries as "the New Prophecy." In fact, if the movement were to be named after its leaders, it might be more appropriate to choose one of a number of women—notably Priscilla and Maximilla—who were arguably more influential than their male colleague. The New Prophecy not only protested against creeping institutionalism and clericalism in the churches but also offered greater freedom for women than in most places.[9]

Montanism has been treated in diverse ways by its contemporaries and historians. Some have regarded it as a heresy, although little evidence of unorthodoxy has been uncovered. Others have hailed it as an early charismatic movement, reviving interest in spiritual gifts that were being marginalized in the mainstream churches. Others again have interpreted it as an early feminist movement. The surviving evidence is too scanty to be definitive, but one of the features of the movement does seem to have been the enfranchisement of all its members to exercise their gifts and participate actively in their gatherings. Although in its early years the revelations of its leading "prophets" were accorded great respect, there was a fundamental conviction that the Spirit had been poured out on all, so all could speak.

The New Prophecy remained strongest, despite increasing opposition, in Phrygia where it began, but it spread quite rapidly across and beyond Asia Minor, attracting crowds to its meetings, winning many fresh adherents, and eventually reaching Rome and North Africa—where it won its most famous recruit, Tertullian. Church leaders were uncertain how to respond to Montanism. It

---

9. For a comprehensive and readable account of the movement, see Christine Trevett, *Montanism: Gender, Authority and the New Prophecy* (Cambridge: CUP, 1996).

worried them as a schismatic movement, but they could not detect clear evidence of heresy. Furthermore, they were aware that its ideas were highly attractive to many members of their own congregations, even if most did not actually join the movement. The apparently inexorable trend toward monovoiced church was by no means enthusiastically welcomed by many who remembered the freedom of earlier years.

The impact of the New Prophecy was double-edged. Although it kept alive memories of multivoiced practices, fear of the movement probably resulted in the churches clamping down on unauthorized participation and exacerbated the move toward institutionalism and clerical control. Despite continued opposition and eventual papal condemnation, the movement persisted until at least the fifth century—sometimes as groups within or on the fringes of the mainstream churches, sometimes as separate communities. But by then the wind was blowing strongly in favor of those who advocated monovoiced church.

The Christendom shift

Much has been written about the impact on the European church (and on Europe) of the adoption of Christianity as the imperial religion by Emperor Constantine I. Although some have rightly insisted that not everything changed in the fourth century as a result of the "Christendom shift"—some of the developments associated with this shift predated it and others evolved slowly afterward—this shift did represent a radical and unanticipated change in the way the church related to the surrounding culture and the way it understood its own role and purpose.[10] One of the consequences was the silencing of the laity. Monovoiced church seemed more appropriate for an imperial institution than the messiness and unpredictability of multivoiced church.

---

10. See Alan Kreider, *The Change of Conversion and the Origin of Christendom* (Harrisburg: Trinity Press, 1999); Stuart Murray, *Post-Christendom* (Carlisle: Paternoster, 2004); and, for an alternative perspective, Peter Leithart, *Defending Constantine* (Downers Grove: IVP, 2010).

A number of factors influenced this development.[11] First, the sheer size of fourth-century congregations inhibited multivoiced participation. Although there are ways of enabling and empowering larger groups to engage in multivoiced worship and learning, this is not as easy or as natural as in smaller communities. Second, the architecture and ambience of the buildings in which Christians now met was very different from the domestic settings of earlier years. If multivoiced church is natural around a meal table, huge basilicas set out as performance spaces or lecture theaters seem to be designed for spectators and monovoiced church.

Third, in the emerging Christendom context the gap that already existed between clergy and laity was widening. Senior clergy especially were becoming powerful political and social dignitaries as well as spiritual leaders. A professional caste was developing, which restricted to its own members an increasing number of functions that in earlier years any church member could have carried out. Fourth, the massive influx into the churches that followed the emperor's identification of himself as a Christian resulted in the catechetical system being overwhelmed. New converts could no longer be inducted through a lengthy, demanding, and life-changing process, which would equip them to be active participants in the churches. There was time now only for rudimentary instruction. Consequently, any attempt to practice multivoiced church in this new environment would struggle to find church members able to participate appropriately.

Fifth, the dominant concern of the emperor appears to have been the unity of the church within a fragmented empire that he was desperate to hold together. Summoning councils, developing unifying creeds, standardizing the New Testament, and discouraging dissent were all ways of achieving this vital goal. Monovoiced church is much more susceptible to clerical, and imperial, control than multivoiced church. Sixth, the marginalization of the gifts of the Spirit, about which Montanists had protested many decades earlier, had continued, depriving multivoiced church of its

---

11. See further Alan Kreider and Eleanor Kreider, *Worship and Mission After Christendom* (Harrisonburg: Herald Press, 2011), 112–115.

energizing diversity. And seventh, as the church became increasingly conscious of its social status and conformed in numerous ways to the norms of classical culture, the influence of rhetoric grew within the churches. Preaching became a highly polished performance art.[12] Congregations became audiences. The emphasis on performance and correct words and procedures inhibited all but those duly qualified from active involvement.

As we have seen, this did not all happen in a single generation. Nor were the changes in practice uniform across the empire. Monovoiced and multivoiced expressions of church were vying with each other before Constantine and there would be multivoiced vestiges in the churches after Constantine. But the Christendom shift ensured that monovoiced church would become and remain dominant.

Protest and recovery

Dominant, certainly, but monovoiced church was not without repeated challenges from those who discovered in their Scriptures a different way of being church and who longed for this in their churches. In protest and renewal movements through the centuries, monovoiced church received trenchant criticism and multivoiced practices were restored. These unauthorized and unregulated practices were some of the features that threatened the control of the church and the state and provoked repression and persecution. "Montanism" was just one of the labels used to discredit these groups. There is space here only to give examples of this recurrent recovery of the vision of multivoiced church.

The Waldensians

The Waldensians were a medieval renewal movement in southern Europe, inspired by the teaching and example of Valdes, a French businessman who, toward the end of the twelfth century, was challenged by Jesus' teaching as he read the Gospels and committed

---

12. See further David Norrington, *To Preach or Not to Preach* (Carlisle: Paternoster, 1996).

himself to voluntary poverty and preaching. He gathered followers from different social classes, but sharing a life of poverty and preaching—the "Poor in Spirit." They formed missionary bands, wore rough clothes, and went around preaching repentance. There were striking similarities between the emphases of Valdes and his near contemporary, Francis of Assisi, but Valdes was treated as a schismatic rather than a saint, and the Waldensians never gained acceptance within the Catholic Church as Francis did.

The Waldensians rejected the monopoly of the clergy. Initially they merely protested against the corruption in the Catholic hierarchy, but as they were excluded and began to develop their own congregations they went further and insisted on the priesthood of all believers, allowing all to preach, teach, and testify. They appointed and trained their own leaders, sending apostles to plant churches in new areas, and relied on traveling pastor-teachers to provide for the needs of scattered groups who had no full-time leaders. But they called these leaders uncles (*barbes*) to distinguish them from the Catholic "fathers," made no distinction between former priests and laypersons, and saw no need to ordain those who provided leadership or to develop hierarchical structures.

Lutz Kaelber, who researched Waldensian communities in various areas, concludes: ". . . lay persons assumed the right, and even the duty, to tell others about the Gospels and to live accordingly." Among the Austrian Waldensians, he adds: "contemporary accounts report that a good layperson, even a woman, if [she or] he knows the words, can procure the Eucharist, of which they partake daily . . . All are called upon to preach and teach, and no one is greater than the others in their community."[13] Waldensians retained the Catholic practice of confession but confessed to one another rather than to a priest.

Gradually, as the movement developed, there were variations within different branches and more structure was introduced. Some groups retained the emphasis on the priesthood of all believers; others appointed leaders for life or senior preachers and the beginnings

---

13. Lutz Kaelber, "Other- and Inner-Worldly Asceticism in Medieval Waldensianism," *Sociology of Religion* 56 (1995): 95, 111.

of a priestly caste or hierarchy are evident. But it is striking that the name of Valdes is the only one commonly associated with this eight hundred-year-old movement. It is difficult to think of any comparable movement that has so few "names" associated with it. The Waldensians were a multivoiced people's movement.[14]

The Lollards

The Lollards were another grassroots movement—this time in medieval England at the end of the fourteenth century. Their inspiration was not a businessman, but an Oxford scholar, John Wyclif, who would surely have been surprised that his strident criticisms of the clergy and many of the practices of the Catholic Church galvanized a movement that not only followed his thinking to its radical conclusions but developed communities that practiced multivoiced church. The movement spread through distributing Bibles and tracts, public preaching, and inviting people to "reading circles."

In an age when people were expected to let the priests do their theological thinking for them, the Lollards encouraged the development of personal Bible study, taught reliance on the Holy Spirit as teacher and guide, and urged members to reach their own decisions on matters of faith rather than accepting ecclesiastical opinions and dogmas. What they wrote and disseminated was designed to provoke discussion rather than promote certain views. Interaction in the reading circles meant that individual responsibility was balanced by communal discernment. Lollards believed that those whose lives were upright—rather than those who were educated and ordained—could anticipate the guidance of the Spirit as they read the Bible together. Rejecting the distinction between clergy and laity, Lollards involved all believers, men and women, in all aspects of church life.

Although the Lollards did not suffer anything like the persecution the Waldensians experienced, their unauthorized gatherings were a persistent irritation to the established church. And their

---

14. See further Malcolm Lambert, *Medieval Heresy* (Oxford: Blackwell, 1992).

criticisms of that church and its priests were often sharp. Their main charge was that the priests "quenched the gifts of the Holy Spirit and blasphemed the Spirit by forbidding men to preach." Their conclusion was that "The Holy Spirit clearly could not be in such men."[15] This assessment would be echoed by later movements that were equally outraged by the restrictions placed on multivoiced church life.

The Anabaptists

The Anabaptists were members of a sixteenth-century radical renewal movement in territories that now comprise parts of Switzerland, Austria, the Czech Republic, Germany, Alsace, and the Netherlands. Its distinguishing features included Christocentrism, emphasis on new birth and discipleship in the power of the Spirit, establishment of believers churches free from state control, commitment to economic sharing and nonviolence, and a vision of restoring New Testament Christianity.

Multivoiced church was a feature of the Anabaptist tradition from the earliest years of the movement. Swiss congregations, meeting in homes or in the open air, encouraged all to participate. Indeed, the expectation was that members were *obliged* to participate if the Spirit prompted them. One of the earliest Anabaptist documents, *The Swiss Order* (1527), explained how they operated: "When brothers and sisters are together, they shall take up something to read together. The one to whom God has given the best understanding shall explain it, the others should be still and listen."[16]

Anabaptists regarded the monovoiced approach of the state churches (both Catholic and Reformed) as inadequate and unspiritual. An early tract complained:

> When someone comes to church and constantly hears only one person speaking, and all the listeners are silent, neither speaking

---

15. Donald Smeeton, "Holy Living and the Holy Ghost: A Study of Wycliffite Pneumatology," *Evangelical Quarterly* 59:2 (1987), 143.
16. Quoted in John Howard Yoder, *The Legacy of Michael Sattler* (Scottdale: Herald Press, 1973), 44.

nor prophesying, who can or will regard or confess the same to
be a spiritual congregation or confess according to 1 Corinthians
14 that God is dwelling and operating in them through his Holy
Spirit with his gifts, impelling them one after the other in the
above mentioned order of speaking and prophesying?[17]

Anabaptists in other parts of Europe adopted a similar multivoiced approach. Ambrosius Spitelmaier, an Anabaptist leader
in Nicholsburg, wrote: ". . . when they come together they teach
each other the divine Word and one asks the others: how do you
understand this saying?"[18] Leopold Scharnschlager, in his *Seven
Articles*, reported that members of Anabaptist congregations in
central Germany stood in turn to read, prophesy, and discuss
Scripture. And disgruntled former Anabaptists in Holland complained about the same multivoiced approach there.[19]

Another dimension of multivoiced church in Anabaptist communities was the practice known variously as "church discipline,"
"the ban," or "the rule of Christ." Baptism into an Anabaptist
congregation meant inviting other members of the community
to exercise "fraternal admonition," "watching over each other in
love," bringing reproof as needed. It was not always exercised
wisely and graciously, but this practice was rooted in both their
reading of the New Testament (Matthew 18:15-18) and their dis-
may at the low standards of discipleship in the state churches. In
a movement that enfranchised its members, some form of community discipline was essential.

These multivoiced church practices may have been less common
in some branches of the movement, especially the communitar-
ian Hutterites, and over the years (as in other renewal movements)
the monovoiced approach seems to have reasserted itself. We do,

---

17. Paul Peachey, "Answer of Some Who Are Called (Ana)Baptists Why
They Do Not Attend the Churches: A Swiss Brethren Tract," *Mennonite
Quarterly Review* (1971), 7. Note the echo of the Lollards' critique.

18. Walter Klaassen, *Anabaptism in Outline* (Scottdale: Herald Press,
1981), 124.

19. See Michael Baylor (ed.), *The Radical Reformation* (Cambridge: CUP,
1991), 224–25.

however, have one fascinating account of multivoiced worship from the late sixteenth century, which suggests that this practice persisted longer than some have assumed. It comes from the pen of a Lutheran minister who infiltrated an Anabaptist gathering in a forest and observed what happened. His description and assessment of what he witnessed needs to be interpreted in light of his hostility to the Anabaptists, but the multivoiced nature of the meeting is very clear. For example, Brother Peter, one of the Anabaptist leaders, addressed the gathering after someone had preached and said: "Now dear brothers, you have heard and understood the Word of God and have prayed earnestly. If there is anyone among you who has not quite understood he should come here and we will instruct him. Or if the Spirit of God reveals anything to someone to edify the brethren, let him come here and we will hear him in a friendly manner."[20]

c/ɔ

Medieval protest movements, however worrying to the authorities, could eventually be suppressed and their scurrilous literature destroyed. The fragmentation of Christendom in the sixteenth century and the availability of printing presses meant that this would be very much harder from now on. We know so much more about the Anabaptists than about the earlier movements. And in the seventeenth century the number and variety of movements seemed to increase exponentially, not least in England.

The English Radicals

The English Radicals is a generic term for many different groups that emerged, disturbed the peace, flourished, declined, or settled down in this turbulent period. Levellers, Fifth Monarchists, Diggers, Ranters, Seekers, Quakers, and Baptists disagreed with one another on many issues, political and theological, but represented (among other things) a further upsurge of protest and

---

20. Elias Schad, "True Account of an Anabaptist Meeting at Night in a Forest and a Debate Held There with Them," *Mennonite Quarterly Review* 58 (July 1984), 292–94.

continuing yearning for a different approach to church life. Multivoiced church was on the agenda again.

Summarizing the conviction of many English radical groups that multivoiced church was necessary and welcome, Christopher Hill concludes:

> Priests and scholars would have liked to keep the interpretation of the Bible the monopoly of an educated elite, as it had been in the days before the vernacular Bible existed. The radical reply was to assert the possibility of any individual receiving the spirit, the inner experience which enabled him to understand God's Word as well as, better than, mere scholars who lacked this inner grace.[21]

As with the Anabaptists, though, personal responsibility was to be exercised in a communal context. Hill continues: "Emphasis on private interpretation was not however mere absolute individualism. The congregation was the place in which interpretations were tested and approved . . . The congregation guaranteed the validity of the interpretation for the given social unit, and was a check on individualist absurdities."[22]

Surveying the complicated scene in seventeenth-century England, Hill provides several examples of multivoiced practices: a Baptist preacher, Mrs. Attaway, encouraging the congregation to ask questions and make objections after hearing her sermon; William Dell insisting that prophesying (by this he meant corrective statements after a sermon) was a "notable means to keep error out of the church"; Henry Denne asserting that it was a rule among the General Baptists "that it shall be lawful for any person to improve their gifts in the presence of the congregation"; Hanserd Knollys creating "several riots and tumults" by going around churches and speaking after the sermon; and the Quakers claiming a legal right to speak after the sermon was over.[23]

---

21. Christopher Hill, *The World Turned Upside Down* (Harmondsworth: Penguin, 1972), 95.
22. Hill, *World*, 95.
23. Hill, *World*, 104–5.

It is reported that Oliver Cromwell instructed the chaplains in his army to ensure that they allowed as much time for questions and comments after their sermons as they had spent preaching them. And Michael Watts notes the influence of 1 Corinthians 14 on John Smyth and the earliest account of Baptist worship (in 1609):

> Smyth's conception of worship, derived from 1 Corinthians 14:30-31, was the spontaneous out-pouring of the Holy Spirit through prophesying, and so the Bible was laid aside and a speaker rose to propound "some text out of Scripture, and prophesieth out of the same, by the space of one hour or three-quarters of an hour." Then a second speaker stood up "and prophesieth out of the said text the like time and space," and after him a third, a fourth, and a fifth "as the time will give leave."[24]

Nineteenth- and twentieth-century movements

The Plymouth Brethren in the nineteenth century and the various Pentecostal and charismatic movements in the twentieth century are more recent examples of the perennial discontent with monovoiced church and the recovery of multivoiced alternatives. In the House Church Movement that flourished in the second half of the twentieth century, especially, 1 Corinthians 14 has been influential, validating and supporting the rediscovery of spiritual gifts such as speaking in tongues, prophecy, and healing, but also encouraging multivoiced participation in worship, if not in all other aspects of church life.

During the past fifty years, despite the persistence of monovoiced patterns of church life, many further explorations of multivoiced church have been emerging. These include cell churches, household churches, simple churches, organic churches, table churches, base ecclesial communities, and many other groups. We will examine these in more detail in subsequent chapters, learning from their experiences, but we should first pause to look back over the story we have told in this chapter and ask what we can learn from these earlier movements, many of which paid a high price for their determination to recover multivoiced church.

---

24. Michael Watts, *The Dissenters* (Oxford: Clarendon, 1978), 74–5.

Stuart grew up in a family that belonged to a Plymouth Brethren assembly that was committed to the priesthood of all (male) believers and multivoiced worship. He recalls Sunday morning services in which there was no designated leader and in which any of the men present could read from the Bible, give an exhortation, pray, or start a song. Any of them could also preside at the weekly communion that was the climax of these services. Inevitably some took part more often than others, and some took part in very predictable ways, despite the underlying assumption that the Spirit would lead and inspire contributions. Stuart's memory is of some wonderfully rich experiences of worship and some that were very dry.

Learning from history

We note first the significance of 1 Corinthians 14—the most extended description in the New Testament of what happened when the early Christians met together, and a passage that abounds in multivoiced practices. References to this chapter are frequent in protest and renewal movements that recovered multivoiced church. But during the Christendom era they are conspicuous by their absence in the mainstream churches. Commentators or liturgical theologians who do cite this chapter tend, as Alan Kreider and Eleanor Kreider note, to concentrate on the restrictions Paul imposes rather than the diverse participation he encourages.[25] Churches today that intend to develop multivoiced practices would do well to explore this passage and learn from it.

Second, most of the multivoiced movements explicitly affirmed the participation of both women and men in some, if not all, dimensions of church life. Even though the prevailing culture in most cases was inimical to this, and even though 1 Corinthians 14 can be read as restricting their vocal participation, the empowerment of women and the adoption of multivoiced practices usually

---

25. Kreider and Kreider: *Worship and Mission After Christendom*, 117.

went hand in hand. We will not argue the case for this in the following chapters; we will simply assume that multivoiced means the same in our churches as it seems to have meant on the Day of Pentecost.

Third, the recovery of multivoiced church in movement after movement seems in most cases to be spontaneous rather than learned from earlier initiatives. There is evidence of limited interaction between some of these movements, especially those which emerged in areas where earlier groups had flourished, but in most cases their beliefs and practices were derived from a fresh encounter with the New Testament and deep discontent with prevailing church culture. Is this an indication of the Spirit's activity and of the power of Scripture to enable God's people to imagine new possibilities? Scanning through church history, as we have done in this chapter, may encourage us to pursue multivoiced church in the knowledge that we have many precedents, but for many groups their understanding of Scripture and what they perceive as the prompting of the Spirit will be enough.

Fourth, many of the movements we have briefly introduced discovered the importance of balancing personal responsibility with communal discernment. Multivoiced church gives great freedom to individuals, but this is open to abuse and can easily result in confusion and disunity. If the contributions of many participants are to build up the church, rather than disturbing it, these need to be weighed by the community and processes need to be developed to enable the community to listen carefully and respond effectively. Both self-discipline and community discipline are vital.

Fifth, what was recovered by one generation was often lost by the next or the one after that. Multivoiced church appears to be easier to recover than to retain. We have already indicated some of the reasons for this.[26] Is there any reason to believe that the prospects are better today? Perhaps there is. As we will see, churches in post-Christendom will no longer be able to operate as they did

---

26. See above in Chapter 1, pp.17–18.

in the Christendom era. In a changing culture and with fewer resources, multivoiced church may be the only expression of church to thrive or even survive. But we will return to this in the final chapter once we have investigated in much more detail how multivoiced church actually operates.

4

Multivoiced Worship

House churches, new churches, emerging churches

In homes up and down the country, in small towns, villages, suburban neighborhoods, even in the inner city, small groups of Christians met to worship together.[1] Some of them still participated in "regular" church on Sundays in consecrated buildings; for others these meetings in homes were "church." Determined to break down the sacred/secular dualism that seemed to characterize "Sunday church," meeting in domestic settings helped them to reconnect their faith with family life, work, leisure, and neighborhood.

Meeting in homes also influenced the way they worshiped together. Weary of formulaic and predictable services, often dominated by professional ministers, organists, and choirs, they yearned for greater spontaneity and joyful celebration. Hearing

---

1. We are fully aware that "worship" is a much broader and richer concept than certain activities that take place when Christians meet together. It is a whole-life response to the presence and purposes of God. But there is a commonly understood and legitimate use of the term to describe some of the things that happen in Christian gatherings. In this chapter, and elsewhere in this book, we use the term in this more restricted sense.

reports of others who had exchanged the organ for guitars, were singing and composing new kinds of songs, and were encouraging everyone to participate, they began to experience a heady new freedom. And the growing influence of charismatic renewal meant that songs, prayers, Bible readings, exhortations, words of encouragement, and testimonies were accompanied by prophecies, words of knowledge, tongues, and interpretations. As in earlier renewal movements, these emerging churches turned to 1 Corinthians 14 for inspiration and guidance.

Between the 1960s and 1980s many hundreds of such communities recovered multivoiced ways of worshiping, trusting that the Holy Spirit would inspire the worshipers and edify the community through their diverse contributions—and for many of those involved this was liberating and life-changing.

This was, of course, the genesis of what became known as the House Church Movement. Some of the communities stagnated, fell out with each other, became introverted and no less formulaic than the churches they had left, or even slipped into heresy. Others grew in numbers and maturity, developed an increasingly missional focus, and faced the challenge of how to manage growth—subdividing to form more house churches or finding spaces in which to gather larger groups. Many moved into schools and community centers, and some, in time, bought or built dedicated church buildings. And as these groups discovered others on similar journeys, networks developed and structures were put in place to serve and resource the communities.

Forty years later and the New Churches (as they are generally now known since most no longer meet exclusively or primarily in houses) are part of the wider church scene. Less distinctive now that many other churches have learned from their experience and drawn on their resources, many of them are also more ecumenically minded and less critical of other expressions of church. The commitment to multivoiced worship remains, in theory and in practice, but there are many signs of reversion to monovoiced practices.

Some of the same influences are apparent as we noted in the previous chapter in relation to the Christendom shift. As numbers grew, multivoiced participation became harder to sustain—partly because fewer people had the courage to speak in a larger community and partly because of concern for quality control in gatherings that had more public exposure. As the communities moved out of homes and into more institutional settings, reversion to monovoiced modes of worship increased. The architecture, acoustics, ambience, and seating arrangements of their meeting places took their toll. As the songs became more complex and harder to play, there was increasing reliance on "worship leaders" and the bands of technically competent musicians they gathered around them. Professionalism had benefits but disempowered the less competent, and severely limited spontaneity and multivoiced participation. And the gifts of tongues, interpretation, and prophecy were exercised less frequently and by fewer people.

Pete Ward, in his book *Selling Worship*, reflects on these issues using the example of the Soul Survivor congregation in Watford, UK. One of its leaders, Mike Pilavachi, realized that the congregation had become "connoisseurs of worship rather than participants in it." The church responded by agreeing to "ban the band" and making space once again for multivoiced worship. Performance had taken priority over participation and this needed to be reined in.[2]

These changes, as in the fourth century, are understandable, and some would conclude that they are signs of maturity. Some of the churches have rediscovered the value of good liturgy and have drawn gratefully on the resources of older churches, often enriching and renewing communities that had become jaded and

---

2. Pete Ward, *Selling Worship* (Milton Keynes: Paternoster, 2005), 171–72, quoting from Mike Pilavachi and Craig Borlase, *For the Audience of One: The Soul Survivor Guide to Worship* (London: Hodder & Stoughton, 1999), 134. See also his reflections on participation and folk art on pp. 183–87 of *Selling Worship*.

uncreative. But in most cases reversion to monovoiced practices has been accidental and unreflective; and there have been losses as well as some gains. And so there are questions:

- What if more had been done to undergird multivoiced practices with a biblical rationale, a historical perspective, and an understanding of the missional potential of multi-voiced worship?

- What if more had been done to teach the principles of multivoiced worship so that any reversion to monovoiced worship could be subjected to proper critique?

- What if more had been done to help multivoiced worshipers mature in their participation and grow in their sensitivity to the Spirit's promptings?[3]

In recent years, much to the chagrin of some of the leaders of these churches, some of those who were brought up in them and others who have come to faith in Christ through their witness have found their ethos, style, and culture uncongenial. Many of these are to be found in the so-called "emerging churches" that represent, among other things, another turn of the wheel and a fresh attempt to recover participatory, multivoiced worship. As with the house churches in the 1960s and 1970s, various local initiatives have gradually become aware that they are part of something bigger—not yet a coherent movement, but seemingly a fresh move of the Spirit.

Some of these groups embrace the phrase "alternative worship"[4]—which, of course, begs the question "to what is this an alternative?" While there are various answers to this, many of those involved are searching for alternatives to the kind of worship

---

3. Stuart was involved for many years in the House Church Movement, starting a church in his home in the late 1970s that grew to a community of around three hundred adults and children and struggled to retain multi-voiced practices, so this section is the critique of an insider, not an outsider.

4. See, for examples, www.alternativeworship.org. For a very helpful discussion, see Doug Gay, *Remixing the Church: Towards an Emerging Ecclesiology* (London: SCM Press, 2011).

they experienced in evangelical charismatic churches that were either New Churches or influenced by them. And while some of the worship practices of these emerging churches are quite different in tone and style from anything in the history of the New Churches, others are restoring aspects of the multivoiced approach that characterized their early years.

We will explore the multivoiced practices of emerging churches in due course (and the criticism from some New Church leaders that these are devoid of the Spirit's inspiration). For now, we note that it was not the multivoiced nature of the New Churches that was rejected but some of the consequences of their reversion to monovoiced practices. The yearning for multivoiced worship appears to be as strong as ever.

What is multivoiced worship?

There is nothing mysterious about the meaning of the term "multivoiced worship." It means simply that when God's people gather, our corporate worship is expressed by many people and in many formats, tones, and accents.[5]

Multivoiced worship anticipates that God may speak or act through any member of the church for the benefit of the whole community. It recognizes that no one person or small group has a monopoly on this. It welcomes the richness and diversity that flow from multiple contributions. It values the different perspectives, insights, angles of vision, experiences, and convictions that different members bring. It does not require that all contribute or that all participate equally; nor is leadership abolished. But the ethos of multivoiced worship is very different from corporate worship that consists of one or very few voices or allows wider participation only through preordained words or actions.

---

5. For a stimulating discussion of multivoiced worship, see Alan Kreider and Eleanor Kreider: *Worship and Mission After Christendom* (Harrisonburg: Herald Press, 2011). Our reflections in this chapter owe much to conversations with the Kreiders.

> Tim Presswood, a Baptist minister working with Urban Expression[6] in Manchester, UK, sent us a blog post from a friend following a recent visit: "I quite liked church this morning . . . I felt like I had something to contribute, I liked the fact that the contributions came from all, including me, and a child, and theologians and scholars and academics . . . the interactive . . . and the quiet, the thinking . . . nobody telling me what I was supposed to think . . . and not much singing."

There are various ways in which multivoiced worship can operate. For example:

- The planning and preparation of corporate worship may involve many people meeting together in advance of when the church gathers.

- When the church gathers, part of the time may be guided by one person and part of the time open to many participants.

- When the church gathers, there may be no obvious leadership but reliance on the Spirit to prompt various members to offer contributions.

- There may be a carefully ordered liturgy which makes room for many voices in both preordained and spontaneous ways.

- There may be occasions when people participate one by one, but other times when the whole community participates in unison.

- When the church gathers, space and time may be allocated for small groups to be creative and to offer what they create within the worship of the whole community.

---

6. See www.urbanexpression.org.uk. Urban Expression, which Stuart founded, is a mission agency working in poor urban communities in Britain and elsewhere.

- In large communities or large meeting places which tend to inhibit multivoiced worship, opportunities may be created for smaller groups to participate within the gathering.

- Contemporary technology makes possible ways of contributing and interacting that, if used sensitively, can empower individuals and enrich the community.

Some of these, and other, expressions of multivoiced worship may already be familiar in our churches. In many communities there are vestiges of past multivoiced practices that can be recovered and renewed, or multivoiced practices in some dimensions of church life that can be extended to others. Very often there is more multivoiced worship in the youth or children's departments than in "adult" church, from which we can learn if we are willing.

Some songs that are written for particular communities cannot be sung with meaning by any other community. In the church just outside Oxford, of which Sian was minister, the church song celebrated the two hundred-year story of the community—with particular reference to events in recent years. The crescendo of one of the verses of this song comes with the line "and the apple tree was dead!" This line is sung with great joy and celebration. No other community that has not been part of this church's story can sing that line in this way—or has the slightest idea of why a dead apple tree is a mark of God's blessing on that church.

Multivoiced worship enables a greater range of gifts to be used to glorify God and edify the church. Our list here is indicative, not exhaustive:

- Poetry, composed beforehand or during the church gathering

- Music played by a soloist or group

- Songs, sung together a cappella or accompanied by a solo instrument or a band

- Songs, sung by a soloist, small group, or choir

- Songs composed by members of the community

Storytelling, very popular in contemporary culture, is also being used increasingly in the churches as an alternative to simply reciting the biblical text. At an Urban Expression leaders' day in Bristol, Chris Sunderland narrated the call of Isaiah (in fact, the whole of Isaiah 6) accompanied by Beethoven's *Egmont Overture*. This poignant passage came alive as we heard afresh the prophetic challenge "Who will go for us?"[7]

- Prayers spoken by individuals

- Praying in unison

- Praise expressed in other tongues

- Interpretations to enable the community to join in

- Singing in tongues in unison

- Bible passages read by an individual, several individuals, or in unison

- Bible passages memorized and narrated or dramatized

---

7. For more on this practice see Chris Sunderland, "Telling Bible in a Prophetic Age," *The Bible in Transmission*, Summer/Autumn 2011, 24–26.

We have been involved in three groups over the past fifteen years that met regularly to enjoy a meal together and share in a "table liturgy." This frames the evening, giving space for conversation and eating together. It contains prayers, Bible readings, opportunities to respond, pauses for reflection, ways of greeting and valuing everyone present, symbolic actions, and the sharing of bread and wine. This is a "leaderless liturgy." Anyone around the table, including children, is free to say any of the words or perform any of the actions.

- Readings from other sources

- Words of exhortation and encouragement

- Prophecies and prophetic actions

- Visions

- Words of knowledge

- Testimonies and stories

Jean had recently become a follower of Jesus. She wanted to express praise to God, but she was not very articulate and, as someone with absolutely no church background, she knew none of the songs her church sang. Nor was she artistic, musical, or much of a reader. But she enjoyed her "keep fit" classes, so she started to use the movements she knew from the classes to express praise and thanksgiving. This was her offering.

- Leaderless liturgies

- Photographic displays

- Artwork, prepared beforehand or created during the church gathering

- Sculpting symbols or bringing symbolic items chosen beforehand

- Audiovisual presentations or playing in the background

- Banners displayed or carried aloft

- Lighting candles or tea lights

- Dance, gestures, or movements

A friend of ours, when he was a local minister, developed a multivoiced approach to celebrating the Lord's Supper. Rather than reading one of the biblical passages that tell the story of Jesus eating the Last Supper with his disciples, he invited the congregation to tell the story to each other. Various people contributed to this, adding details that filled out the story. And the story came alive in fresh ways.

- Processions, labyrinths, and prayer stations

- Greeting each other or "passing the peace"

- Washing one another's feet

- Laying on of hands for prayer, healing, or commissioning

- Anointing with oil

- Sharing bread and wine

- Eating together

- Bringing monetary and other gifts

Again, some of these practices may already be familiar within some of our churches and, with encouragement, could be further developed. Others may sound uncomfortable, alien, or disturbing. Exploring these will take us out of our comfort zone. The potential of some to enrich corporate worship may be obvious, but we may not immediately see the point of other practices.

But multivoiced worship is not simply about diversity of practices but about the many different members of the community finding their voices and bringing their offerings. A multifaceted gathering for worship can enrich the community; but empowering all, or at least many, to contribute edifies all those who contribute as well as those who gratefully receive these contributions.

> **Trisha Dale describes the "Corinthian services" her church sometimes holds:**
>
> These came from a discussion on worship we held over a lunch after church one Sunday a couple of years ago. The name is taken from the text in Corinthians about "when you gather, each one has a . . ." People are told in advance (about three weeks) that such a service will be held, and to let whoever is leading it know what they are likely to bring. This is often a choice of hymn/song, Bible reading, etc. but has also included poetry, dramatic readings involving two or three people, and testimonies. We don't announce a theme in advance, but often a strong theme emerges during the service. People sometimes spontaneously make contributions, stimulated by something that has been included.

Multivoiced worship welcomes the very different contributions of the young and the old, the mature disciple and the new believer, women and men, people from different ethnic, social, and cultural backgrounds. Multivoiced communities believe that sometimes "a little child will lead them."[8] It is perhaps within "alternative worship"

---

8. Isa 11:6.

communities that the widest range of contributions has been valued in recent years. Jonny Baker advocates the opening up of attitudes to worship "so that poets, photographers, ideas people, geeks, theologians, liturgists, designers, writers, cooks, politicians, architects, moviemakers, storytellers, parents, campaigners, children, bloggers, DJs, VJs, craft-makers, or just anybody who comes and is willing to bounce ideas around, can get involved."[9]

Many gatherings for worship seem to be dominated by a "tyranny of joyfulness"—an expectation that everyone is full of the joy of the Lord all the time. Multivoiced worship is not oppressed and homogenized in this way. When responsibility for leading worship rests with very few people and there is little scope for interjections, the range of emotions is generally very limited. Multivoiced worship, by contrast, gives scope for many different people to express a wider range of emotions—anger, outrage, grief, hurt, confusion, longing, awe, hesitancy, hope, compassion, quiet acceptance—as well as exuberance and celebration. Not only does this result in richer worship, but it is a more authentic expression of the life of the worshiping community. And including testimonies and reports of experiences with God during the past week helps to ensure worship is not disconnected from daily life.

> Trevor Withers reports that in the Network Church, St. Albans, UK, they give at least twenty minutes in each service to hearing how people have been experiencing God (or not) in their week. This is done by sitting next to people in their seats with a radio mike so it is not an upfront performance.

But isn't multivoiced worship risky? Yes. Isn't it often messy? Yes. Some contributions may not be as edifying and uplifting as others. They may not flow together as effectively as a carefully crafted monovoiced service might. And this kind of freedom to

---

9. Jonny Baker, *Curating Worship* (London: SPCK, 2010), 12. A VJ is a "video jockey," similar to a DJ but using video clips, etc.

participate can be abused. Attention seeking, self-indulgence, banality, incoherence—these may all characterize multivoiced worship (and, for that matter, monovoiced worship!).

All of which means that communities intent on exploring and practicing multivoiced worship need to be realistic about the challenges as well as hopeful about the potential. Patience and perseverance will be required, as well as a commitment to learn together. Except on rare occasions, exhilarating multivoiced worship does not just happen. What is needed is an *ethos* that is conducive to developing such a community, *ground rules* that provide both security and clarity, and *processes* to help a multivoiced community mature.

Phil Warburton writes that in E1 Community Church, a Baptist church in East London planted by an Urban Expression team and strongly influenced by the Anabaptist tradition, the questions regularly asked are: "How was your week—where was God in it? Can you name one thing you are grateful for? One thing you're finding difficult?"

Creating an ethos

Whether the starting point is a newly planted church that has no established pattern yet of worshiping together, or a predominantly monovoiced church that is journeying toward a more multivoiced expression, creating an ethos within which multivoiced worship can flourish is vital. The community needs to understand what multivoiced worship is, how it differs from monovoiced worship, and why the church is embracing this. Reassurance that this is authentically biblical and has many historical precedents may be important in sustaining initial enthusiasm. Creating an ethos of exploring, experimenting, freedom to make mistakes, learning together, and persevering in spite of disappointments is crucial if the church is to overcome setbacks, refuse to take itself too seriously, and resist the drag back into monovoiced worship.

Churches that want to develop and sustain multivoiced worship will do well to establish the principle of multivoiced worship within their core values and regularly rehearse this in their gatherings. Once again we need to stress that the default position is monovoiced and that reverting to this approach will only be resisted with persistence and care. If being multivoiced is one of the core values of a church, recognized by the church as an aspect of its community identity, this is more likely to persist.

> Being a multivoiced community is one of the core values of E1 Community Church. Church members regularly remind themselves that this is who they are: "The Holy Spirit gives all followers of Jesus the strength and ability to do God's work. We believe that God doesn't just speak through professional church people. We need to listen to each other to hear what God has to say. This value will be reflected in how we worship and make decisions."

Creating this kind of ethos, or climate, requires gentle but firm leadership. Most of those who experiment with "leaderless" worship in the hope that this will encourage multiple participation tend fairly soon to revert to some form of leadership. Multivoiced worship does not abolish the need for skillful leadership, but it redefines the role and priorities of those who lead. Leadership of multivoiced gatherings will be facilitative, empowering, and encouraging, making space for many to participate and for all to benefit. Alternative worship communities sometimes speak of "worship curators" rather than worship leaders, comparing their role to that of curators of art exhibitions: "A worship curator makes a context and a frame for worship, arranging elements in it. The content is provided by other people."[10]

Church members need to know that there is freedom to step out in faith, to dare to make a contribution, to speak out rather

---

10. Baker, *Curating*, xiv.

than remain silent, and that those with leadership responsibilities will be supportive, honest, and gracious as they "equip [God's] people for works of service."[11] In particular, an ethos conducive to multivoiced worship involves:

- A spirit of generosity that looks first for what is good in any contribution rather than for any inadequacies.

- A spirit of adventure that encourages risk taking, creativity, and exploration rather than the "safety first" ethos that stymies so many communities.

- A spirit of humility that acknowledges we are all learning and that we need one another's help, encouragement, and constructive criticism.

- A spirit of encouragement that spurs one another on when the community begins to question whether the journey is worth it.

It is important for the community to talk together about the practicalities of multivoiced worship. Time needs to be set aside to reflect together on their experiences of this, good and bad, so that the community is learning how to take part and respond more effectively. Those who lead the church can encourage an ethos of reflection on what works well and less well. And if multivoiced worship is to be embedded in the church, those who join need to be inducted into this ethos, so that they understand what this means and why it is important to the church. Newcomers also need to be encouraged to find their voices.

> In E1 Community Church, thirty suggestions of how people might participate in worship are laid out on cards on the floor. Members of the church are invited to come forward, pick a card, and do what it suggests. Another way of encouraging timid members is to invite everyone to fill in the blank in a simple prayer or statement, such as "Not even . . . can separate us from the love of God."

11. Eph 4:12.

There are some practical steps we can take to create an ethos within which multivoiced worship is more likely to thrive and be sustained. We can meet in a domestic setting if our community is small enough or reproduce some aspects of such a setting in a larger gathering. A friend of ours leads a church that has a working fireplace in the otherwise quite traditional building where the church gathers. Many emerging churches make use of sofas, beanbags, café-style tables and chairs, and other less formal furniture. Some seating arrangements are more conducive to multivoiced worship than others—and communities may need to experiment with various possibilities until they find one that works well for them. In larger gatherings and buildings, we need to think carefully about how people can be heard if they participate.

> Marg Hardcastle, an Urban Expression mission partner in Stoke, UK, has found a way to help church members who are willing to participate but are not particularly confident to take a whole service. They have developed a "DIY Service Pack," which involves breaking the service (and the "sermon slot") into small parts and allocating responsibility for each part. This has built confidence and has meant people spending more time together thinking and preparing.

Churches that are transitioning from monovoiced to multivoiced worship may find it helpful to make changes that de-emphasize certain roles and challenge assumptions. For example, situating the musicians to the side or even at the back rather than at the front; leading worship from the heart of the congregation rather than at the front; configuring the meeting space so that there is no "front"; or meeting in the round rather than in rows facing in one direction. Arranging the seating so that members of the church can see and interact with each other is more conducive to multivoiced worship. If there is no obvious "front," it is harder for monovoiced worship to be reestablished. One way of reinforcing the commitment to multivoiced worship might be to display sections of 1 Corinthians 14 in the space where the church meets and refer to this regularly.

Susan Williams is one of the founders of Christ Church Deal (UK), an evangelical church that is also a recognized therapeutic community. She told us that since the church began in 1998, multivoiced worship has characterized their gatherings. The worship group always plays from the back of the hall and the congregation is often in a semicircle with nobody obviously leading. There is a microphone in the middle and everyone is encouraged to participate actively. Space is left between songs for people to sing out their own extemporary words or phrases, individually and in harmony. The founding vision of the church was to be "a safe space for people who are hurting," and multivoiced worship with freedom for all to take part has contributed to this.

Establishing ground rules

As in many areas of life, the freedom implicit in multivoiced worship thrives in a context of security. Structures and ground rules provide the necessary frameworks for creativity. Multivoiced worship might be compared to musical improvisation, in which knowledge of the rules of music and sensitivity to other instrumentalists ensures that the result is not cacophony. Establishing ground rules for multivoiced worship helps to express the ethos that we are creating and to embed it in the community. These rules are not impositions on a community but agreed-upon practices that themselves emerge out of multivoiced processes.[12] They help to build trust in the community.

Each community that commits itself to multivoiced worship will need to establish rules and practices that are appropriate in its own context, but 1 Corinthians 14 indicates the kinds of issues that might be addressed:

- A limitation on the number of times anyone can participate. This is to prevent the dominance of a few voices and

---

12. On which, see Chapter 8.

open up opportunities for others who may be less confident or slower to step forward—"you can all prophesy in
turn."[13] The agreed limit might apply to each gathering
(two or at most three contributions, for example) or to
all the gatherings in a certain period (say, four times in a
month).

• A commitment to "weigh carefully what is said."[14] This
may involve pausing from time to time, or after particular
contributions, to reflect carefully on what has been heard
or seen. This practice is important for several reasons. It
helps to ensure that contributions are treated with respect
and that the community is edified by them, rather than
rushing on. It gives confidence to those who take part that
what they bring matters—and that if they make mistakes
this will not damage or distract the community. And it
gives opportunity for some reorientation in the direction
of the meeting if this is necessary.

• An open invitation to others in the community to offer
feedback—encouragement and critique—so that "everyone may be instructed and encouraged."[15] This needs to
be handled carefully, of course, and we may want to be
explicit about when and how such feedback is offered. And
any feedback needs to be offered in the spirit of the ethos
the community has created.

• A commitment to provide an explanation of what is
happening for any newcomers or visitors. Those who are

---

13. 1 Cor 14:31. In this section Paul offers ground rules to ensure that
the gifts of tongues, interpretation, and prophecy are exercised in ways
that will build up the church, but the principles apply equally to other
forms of participation.
14. 1 Cor 14:29. Similarly Paul tells the Thessalonians not to treat
prophecies with contempt but to test everything and hold on to the
good (1 Thess 5:20-21).
15. 1 Cor 14:31.

unfamiliar with what happens in church gatherings (in post-Christendom an increasing number) need to be made welcome and invited to participate or simply observe. Those who are familiar with monovoiced worship may need a similar explanation and invitation.[16]

A familiar liturgical framework may provide an ideal context for multivoiced worship. It is important that we do not equate multivoiced worship with absence of structure in our gatherings. Most communities do in fact develop a liturgical structure, even if this is not explicit or acknowledged, so a liturgical framework that is understood and valued is generally more helpful. This can be very simple or quite complex. What matters is that the community understands the structure and learns how multivoiced elements relate to this.

> Tim Foley, a colleague in the Anabaptist Network who lives in Portadown, Northern Ireland wrote to us about the monthly Celtic eucharist at Armagh Church of Ireland cathedral. "It involves a thirty-minute Celtic eucharist and liturgy followed by a simple Christian Aid lunch. The liturgy is Celtic, from the usual sources, yet is almost all multivoiced, with the priest leading us in prayers and response. It feels like work, the work of the people (liturgy)."

Common liturgical elements include: a call to worship; praise and thanksgiving; an act of confession; reading and reflecting on Scripture; sharing communion; bringing offerings; intercessory prayers; and commissioning or benediction. Other elements are the sharing of news and testimonies; ministry to one another; waiting upon God; and greeting one another. Some communities may add further regular activities. Others may have a much simpler structure (such as praise, preaching, ministry time). Multivoiced worship is not precluded by these elements or by a familiar order

---

16. 1 Cor 14:23-25. Paul expresses concern that visitors encounter the presence of God rather than experiencing confusion and uncertainty.

or structure; rather, this framework can help worshipers to partici-pate in ways that are appropriate and edifying.

Giving thought to how a worshiping event unfolds in a way which both holds meaning and proclaims good news is important. Multivoiced worship does not envisage a random sequence of "items" offered. A rich experience of worship takes worshipers on a "liturgical journey" through the event, as they encounter a God who journeys with them. Such an experience has been described as enjoying a lavish five-course banquet, leaving the diner enriched, nourished, sated. Deep worship is not a grazing time, but involves feasting with Christ.

So if a multivoiced worshiping community understands the "liturgical journey" they are on when they meet together, and if they are familiar enough with the framework not to have to con-centrate too much on this, they can learn to participate in ways that are both "fitting and orderly."[17] At appropriate points different voices can offer prayers of praise, bring words of encouragement, sing a lament, retell part of the biblical story, or share a testimony. Without this framework multivoiced worship can be diffuse, even chaotic. But, as with musical improvisation, an agreed but flex-ible structure can release creativity and result in an extraordinary harmony.

> We both visit many churches in the course of a year and we participate in services that have more or less explicit liturgical frameworks. But in many congregations there seems little awareness of the "liturgical journey," and the worship (monovoiced or multivoiced) often feels impoverished and lacking in direction. The problem is often exacerbated by an insatiable appetite among the musicians to teach new songs, many of them remarkably similar to older songs, that hinder the congregation from relaxing into familiar words and tunes and being able to concentrate on God rather than the songs.

---

17. 1 Cor 14:40.

Learning and growing

Our brief survey in the previous chapter of movements that rediscovered multivoiced worship included several that reverted to
monovoiced worship in later generations, albeit sometimes with
vestiges of their earlier practice. But within some traditions multivoiced worship has persisted much longer.

The Society of Friends (Quakers) continues to practice a multivoiced form of worship,[18] although often in their gatherings silence
is more evident than many voices contributing. But the understanding of the worshipers is that they should speak when the Spirit
urges them to do so. Many Christian Brethren assemblies also continue to practice multivoiced worship, at least in their communion
services, and some have extended the scope of this practice, rather
than restricting it. Women are now welcome to contribute in some
of their churches, and a wider range of spiritual gifts can also sometimes be found.

However, these traditions have struggled in other ways with
multivoiced worship. It may theoretically be possible for all to participate but in practice relatively few do—and often they participate
in predictable ways. Multivoiced worship can become moribund,
banal, and uncreative. The problem may not be disorder, as in
Corinth, but the result is equally unedifying. It is important, therefore, that we identify some of the common problems that churches
committed to multivoiced worship encounter and recognize the
need to keep learning and growing.

Common problems that develop in churches practicing multivoiced worship include:

- Despite encouragements to the reluctant, and quiet
  words with the overzealous, the same voices are heard frequently and others only rarely, if at all.

- Some of those who take part tend to do so in ways that
  are predictable, verging on the formulaic, rather than
  remaining open to the Spirit's creativity.

---

18. Not all Quakers have retained this practice. Some have reverted to a
more programmatic approach.

• The range of different kinds of contributions diminishes until songs and prayers are all that remains from the smorgasbord of gifts previously brought to the table.

• Some of those who participate seem poorly attuned to others or to the "liturgical journey" and contribute in ways that seem out of step and ill timed.

• Imbalance between contributions that are directed toward God (prayer, tongues and interpretation, most songs, etc.) and contributions directed toward the church (prophecy, exhortations, biblical readings, testimonies, etc.).

• Multivoiced worship becomes confused with "spontaneous" worship, and when this becomes prevalent the quality tends to suffer badly. Prayerful preparation of ourselves and our contributions will greatly enhance multivoiced worship.

• Limited focus on the world beyond the church and the mission of God in which the church is invited to participate, and inadequate connections between worship and everyday life.

• Despite the judicious use of technology and gentle encouragement, some mumble their contributions, making it difficult for others to benefit from what is said.

• Church members with busy lives and demanding jobs struggle to find time and energy to prepare adequately and hanker after less participative worship.

• Newcomers who have experience of monovoiced churches advocate reverting to the dominant practice, often in the name of "higher quality" or "attractiveness to outsiders."

There are ways in which communities that are committed to persisting with multivoiced worship can address these issues:

- Regularly reviewing progress and talking together about problems they encounter;

- Confronting concerns relating to particular individuals through gracious pastoral conversations;

- Providing regular training and encouragement to explore creative possibilities;

- Modeling good practice from which others can learn;

- Reverting to monovoiced worship for a limited trial period so that the community can discover what it is missing; or

- Simply pressing through times of discouragement without being knocked off course.

And, of course, some of these problems are common in monovoiced churches, too!

But the vitality and richness of multivoiced worship depends not only on commitment to this as a core value, skillful leadership, ongoing training, and willingness to address issues that are hindering the church. Above all, it depends on the vitality of the spiritual life of the worshipers, who are together responsible for creating corporate worship. There is no room to hide, as there is in monovoiced churches, behind a few spiritual superstars. This is the heart of multivoiced worship. This is why it is hard to sustain but also why it is so valuable. Multivoiced worship is a barometer of the spiritual life of a church in a way that monovoiced worship can never be.

It is important that communities committing themselves to multivoiced worship see this as an ongoing journey rather than something that can be achieved and established. There will be much to learn, and unlearn, as the journey proceeds.

Conclusion

So is it worth the effort if multivoiced worship throws up so many problems? Maybe there are good reasons why this keeps reverting to monovoiced worship! We will return to this question in the final chapter, in which we will review this and other multivoiced practices, but we end this chapter with a few anticipatory comments.

Is multivoiced worship worth introducing and persisting with? It depends on how crucial we think this is—biblically, pastorally, missionally, and spiritually. It depends on how we assess the constant rediscovery of this practice through church history. It depends on how we read our culture and whether we think monovoiced or multivoiced worship is more likely to engage our contemporaries. It depends on our own experience of multivoiced and monovoiced worship and the impact on our own lives as followers of Jesus.

5

Multivoiced Learning

In praise of preaching

We are going to raise many concerns in this chapter about the place of preaching in the churches. We are going to be critical of the dominance of monologue communication. We are going to advocate a much more multivoiced approach to learning in the Christian community. We are going to suggest that preachers and congregations learn new skills and discover new ways of wrestling with Scripture and applying its teaching to our lives. In fact, we are going to be so trenchant in our critique of the status quo in many churches that some might think we no longer believe in preaching at all.

So let us state at the outset that we do believe in preaching. We have both preached many hundreds of sermons—devotional, thematic, narrative, evangelistic, expositional. Stuart planted and led a church in East London for twelve years, in which he preached regularly, including many series of sermons. Sian preached on most Sundays during the five years she was the minister of a church on the outskirts of Oxford. We have both preached in numerous other churches of diverse sizes, styles, and denominations, at conferences and assemblies, and in several countries. Sian now teaches preaching to Baptist ministerial students and Anglican ordinands in Bristol.

And we have, of course, listened to thousands of sermons in all kinds of contexts. Most we have long forgotten; some had a profound impact on our lives; many others inspired, encouraged, and challenged us at the time, even if we no longer recall them. We know that the Spirit of God does remarkable things through preachers and their sermons. And we honor those who preach, for their attentiveness to God's Spirit, their gifts and skills in communicating, and the sheer hard work of preparing sermons.

But how does preaching relate to the multivoiced approach to church we are advocating throughout this book? And why do we question a practice that has been familiar to many generations of Christians and is of central importance in many churches (especially those in the evangelical and Reformed traditions)?

Problems with preaching

We have heard several people comment that sermons in the churches are the last bastions of unchallengable monologues in contemporary culture. Nowhere else does one person speak at length to a silent and passive audience that has no expectation or opportunity of engaging with the speaker. Actually, we are not persuaded that sermons are maintaining this tradition alone. There are other examples in tertiary education, politics, and business. But these are increasingly rare, so monologue sermons seem somewhat out of step with social, educational, and cultural developments.

Thirty years ago Klaus Runia, in his book *The Sermon Under Attack*,[1] which is a spirited defense of sermons and a plea for more effective preaching, explored some of the reasons why monologue preaching was subject to criticism. He identified three shifts that were already underway—and have become much more apparent since then:

---

1. Klaus Runia, *The Sermon Under Attack* (Carlisle: Paternoster, 1983).

- A *cultural* shift from passive instruction to participatory learning, paternalism to partnership, monologue to dialogue, instruction to interaction.

- A *societal* shift from an integrated world to a world where networks overlap, a shift from simplicity to complexity, from stability to rapid change.

- A *media* shift from linear to nonlinear methods of conveying information, from logical argument to pick-'n'-mix learning, from words to images.

These shifts, Runia argues, present significant challenges to preachers. We are operating in a different context than previous generations of preachers. Most of those who listen to sermons today are used to questioning and challenging what they hear, expect to engage with visual as well as verbal stimuli, assume that they have something to contribute to the learning process, and welcome diverse perspectives rather than authoritative statements.

> Years ago at school, studying the causes of World War I, Stuart remembers being given an authoritative list to learn and reproduce in a test. A generation later he remembers his son Robert studying the same subject—confronted by a range of sources (contemporary speeches, political cartoons, newspaper articles, the views of different historians)—and being invited to discern for himself what were the causes of the conflict.

How might preachers respond? Recognizing that the fundamental hope of preaching is that the living, creating, word of God is proclaimed and inspires transformation—from conversion, to deepened following of Jesus, to a complete change of life direction—with what can multivoiced preaching gift us? We might embrace the idea of partnership and encourage much more active participation as preacher and congregation together reflect on Scripture and its application. Preachers bring distinctive contributions to this discernment process, drawing on their training, research, and prayerful preparation. But members of the church can bring other contributions if they are empowered and encouraged to do so.

We might recognize the need for many voices as we attempt to apply biblical insights and theological principles to a complex and rapidly evolving society. Members of the church will have expertise on a wide range of issues that preachers do not. Their voices need to be heard if connections are to be made between Scripture and the worlds of work, leisure, politics, education, neighborhood, family, and daily life.

We might explore alternatives to the monologue sermon, making judicious use of visual media and making room for different perspectives to be presented. Some of our sermons might be exploratory and open ended, rather than the last word on the subject. We might invite dialogue and debate, especially on subjects on which Christians disagree. Sermons might form only one component in a multifaceted learning program.

It has been encouraging to hear of many preachers and churches that have recognized the significance of these issues and have begun to embrace the challenge of moving from monovoiced to multivoiced learning. But others have been much more reluctant and have responded instead by defending traditional forms of preaching and the dominant role of monologue sermons in the churches. They have argued:

- "Preaching has nurtured and sustained the churches for many centuries, so we should not tinker with such a central practice."

- "Preaching is a biblical mandate, which we are not at liberty to dispense with, downgrade, or marginalize."

- "Preaching is a sacrament, an encounter with God. Its effectiveness cannot be assessed like other forms of communication."

- "Preaching provides authoritative proclamation, which may today be uncongenial but is essential if the church is to present a clear witness."

- "Preaching has changed over recent decades and is now much better suited to the contemporary cultural context."

- "Questioning preaching is yet another example of kowtowing to culture shifts and retreating from authentic biblical practices."

We have some sympathy with all of these responses and we have attempted to take them seriously in this chapter and elsewhere. In particular, we acknowledge that preaching has a mysterious dimension (which some would call sacramental) and that treating sermons merely as a mode of communication and subjecting them to critique on educational or cultural grounds misses something very important. Furthermore, we agree that there is a place for authoritative proclamation in the churches and that in particular contexts and at certain times monovoiced sermons have enduring value. And we acknowledge that there have been many changes in the way preaching is understood and practiced in recent years (not least through the "New Homiletic"[2]).

We are also very aware of the danger of "kowtowing to culture shifts." This is a perennial temptation. Christians through the centuries have wrestled with the relationship between gospel and culture, striving to avoid compromise on the one hand and irrelevance on the other. Fresh challenges arise when the gospel breaks into different cultures. Missionaries are confronted by beliefs, practices, structures, customs, and systems that require them to reflect afresh on biblical teaching and the historic practices of the churches. And fresh challenges also arise when culture shifts take place within societies in which the churches have long

---

2. See, for example, Fred Craddock, *As One Without Authority* (Nashville: Abingdon, 1979); Eugene Lowry, *The Homiletical Plot: The Sermon as Narrative Art Form* (Louisville, KY: Westminster/John Knox Press, 2001).

been established and in which questions about the relationship between gospel and culture had apparently been resolved in previous generations.

The most prominent features of the culture shift taking place in all Western societies are commonly identified as "post-modernity" and "post-Christendom." These terms suggest that the rationalistic and optimistic culture of modernity that has dominated our society for the past three centuries is losing coherence, and that we no longer live in a "Christian society" in which the biblical narrative is known and believed or in which the church has a central role.[3] This culture shift has been accompanied by a sustained decline in the size, number, and influence of the churches, which now comprise a small minority in a society frequently regarded as secular but also influenced by other forms of spirituality and other religious traditions.

How do we respond? Do we interpret this culture shift as hostile to the gospel and hold firm to our long-established convictions, customs, and practices, confident that these do not need to be renegotiated or even reexamined? Do we embrace it enthusiastically and allow emerging cultural norms to overturn our previous theological, ethical, and ecclesial norms? Or do we engage critically with this culture shift, welcoming it as an opportunity to reflect carefully on the attempts of previous generations to contextualize the gospel in their cultures? We suggest that this third response is the most promising.

In relation to preaching, this means that we do not abandon the practice just because our culture reacts badly to authoritative and unchallengable monologues, but that we seize the chance to reexamine the biblical and historical evidence and are free to ask whether our forebears might themselves have been guilty of "kowtowing to culture" in the way in which they practiced preaching.

---

3. There is a huge literature of post-modernity and a growing literature on post-Christendom. If you are unfamiliar with these terms, you might start with Stanley Grentz, *A Primer on Postmodernism* (Grand Rapids: Eerdmans, 1996) and Stuart Murray, *Post-Christendom* (Carlisle: Paternoster, 2004).

In previous chapters we have already presented some of the evidence. Monologues can be found in the Bible but are nothing like as prominent as they are in many churches today, and the biblical narrative offers many examples of other forms of communication. In the early churches sermons were preached, but there are numerous examples of multivoiced learning, and the domestic context ensured dialogue was more common than monologue.

The dominance of the monologue sermon can be traced to the Christendom shift, during which the clergy became more powerful, the laity lost their voice, congregations grew in size, the architecture of church buildings discouraged participation, spiritual gifts were marginalized, and the failure of the catechetical system made it difficult to sustain multivoiced church life.

Another feature of this previous culture shift, mentioned only in passing earlier, was the growing desire of church leaders—now feted and financed by the empire—to conform to the norms of classical culture. In this culture the art of rhetoric was highly regarded, with trained and skilled orators receiving huge popular acclaim. Given its heightened status in society, surely the church also needed to produce brilliant orators to match the pagans. It could no longer tolerate the very mixed quality of multivoiced participation.

And so the emphasis shifted from participation to performance—disempowering all but the orators—and from learning to teaching. Ironically, the Latin word *sermo*, from which we derive our word "sermon," and the Greek word *homilia*, which has given us the term "homily," both originally meant "a conversation" (!), but monologues came to dominate the fourth-century churches. Are we wrong to interpret this as an example of an earlier generation of Christians "kowtowing to culture"? Might our current culture shift be an opportunity to revisit this and reexamine the role of preaching in our churches?

The difficulty is that monovoiced preaching is so well established in the churches. Even in the medieval period, when sermons were often absent, monovoiced church life was normal, with passive and silent laity watching the clergy perform. When the Reformers insisted on preaching as one of the marks of the true church, the sermon was restored to its fourth-century centrality, but critics noted that the monopoly of the priest had simply been replaced by the monopoly of the preacher. Protestant churches are usually as monovoiced as Catholic or Orthodox churches, or even more so. We have noted many examples of multivoiced learning through the centuries and in recent first-generation movements, reminders that there is an alternative tradition from which to learn and draw inspiration, but the central place of preaching and the monovoiced approach are so deeply rooted in many churches that any challenge produces substantial resistance.

So, even if questioning the role of preaching is not an example of "kowtowing to culture" but a reminder that its dominant position is the result of a much earlier compromise with culture, is it worth persisting in the face of such resistance? Is the continued dominance of monovoiced preaching damaging the churches and their witness?

We believe it is. Regardless of whether our culture responds well or badly to monologue presentations, we have serious concerns about the impact on the churches of relying so heavily on sermons:

- Research into the effectiveness of sermons has uncovered worrying evidence that we need to take seriously. North American and European studies have produced similar results: somewhere between 65 percent and 90 percent of those interviewed directly after the meeting ended could not say what the main point of the sermon was or what issue it was addressing.[4] We have acknowledged that sermons impact us in other ways than merely conveying information, but this is still worrying.

- People have different learning preferences, so over-reliance on one method of teaching disadvantages those who do not find monologue preaching accessible. Sermons

---

4. For example, see Joani Schultz and Thom Schultz, *Why Nobody Learns Much of Anything at the Church: And How to Fix It* (Loveland, Colorado, Group Publishing: 1993).

communicate well with some, but our congregations are increasingly composed of those who have learned to learn in different ways.

• The dominance of monologue sermons produces passive consumers rather than active participants in learning. This disempowers and deskills congregations. It is not surprising that biblical illiteracy and the inability to reflect theologically are rampant in our churches.

• We place unrealistic demands on those who preach regularly. We expect them to produce week by week sermons that inspire, encourage, challenge, equip, instruct, motivate, comfort, and transform those who listen. We are locked into a paradigm that requires greater skill than most preachers have. The orators the fourth-century preachers aspired to emulate were exceptional, brilliant communicators. We have a few such preachers today, but most of us are somewhere on the scale of duff to average. We prepare prayerfully and conscientiously; we preach faithfully and as well as we can; we learn from our experiences and from others; and we hope to improve. Just occasionally we produce an outstanding sermon, but we don't know how to stay on this level. We would benefit from preaching less often, and our churches would benefit from other forms of learning.

• We hear more sermons than we can possibly respond to properly. Would reducing the number of sermons dishonor preaching or enhance its significance? Maybe if we had fewer sermons and more opportunities to engage with them, process them together, explore their implications, and apply them to our lives, we would benefit more from them and treat them with greater respect.

We believe that these concerns, together with the biblical and historical evidence we have presented and several features of our cultural context, require us to reconsider the role of preaching in our churches. Before we conclude this chapter we will address objections to what we are proposing—reducing our reliance on monovoiced sermons, shifting the emphasis from preaching to learning, and developing a wider range of learning processes. But we hope we have said enough to persuade at least some of our readers that it is worth exploring multivoiced alternatives and other ways of building learning communities.

Jeremy Thomson writes:

For all the effort of preparing, delivering, and listening to sermons, most church members are not as mature as we might expect as a result. Why is this? Of course, there are bad sermons, and there are preachers whose lives are inconsistent with their teaching. But people may listen week by week to the best prepared and presented sermons, given by thoroughly sincere preachers, and yet make little progress in Christian discipleship. Some preachers blame congregations for a lack of expectancy that God will speak, for an inability to listen to a "solid exposition," or even for disobedience to what they hear. But I suspect that there is a more significant factor in the failure rate of the sermon than the quality of the preacher or the responsiveness of the hearers. I want to suggest that the problem lies in our concept of preaching itself.[5]

Multivoiced learning

In this section we offer examples of multivoiced approaches to learning. Some of these represent only minimal changes to what is normal in many monovoiced churches. They are low-risk initiatives that are not likely to provoke great resistance. Others will require greater imagination, courage, and persistence if churches are to learn how to learn in fresh ways. Some will be effective only if preachers and congregations are willing to learn and practice new skills. Many of the practices we suggest will work in most communities, but some are more appropriate in smaller or larger

---

5. Jeremy Thomson: *Preaching as Dialogue: Is the Sermon a Sacred Cow?* (Nottingham: Grove Books, 1996), 3.

churches, in younger or older churches, in more formal or informal congregations. We also need to consider our social context and the cultural ethos of the church (for example, nonbook congregations will not respond well if people are expected to read texts). None of the practices will appeal to everyone—but monologue sermons don't either!

Underlying all of these examples are three foundational principles:

- They are *learner oriented*, concerned more about what is learned than what is taught, more about the outcomes than the methodology, more about stimulating growth in discipleship than oratorical skill or sermon-crafting proficiency.

- They are *multivoiced*, inviting many people to participate in a dialogue rather than listening to a monologue. They assume that nobody has a monopoly on revelation or wisdom and that there are resources in the congregation that will enable Scripture to be understood and applied more effectively if these can be released.

- They are *open ended*, prepared to leave loose ends, to run the risk of allowing people space to think, reflect, explore, and ask how biblical teaching might apply to their situations. They offer resources rather than rules, see discipleship as a journey rather than a fixed state, pose questions rather than dispensing answers, and invite ownership rather than imposing conclusions.

Here, then, is a selection of practices that will enable churches to become more multivoiced and mature as learning communities. All of these are practices that we have used ourselves or know others have used.

Pause for reflection

Congregations that for years have sat passively listening to sermons can be invited to find their voices and engage more actively in the learning process if the preacher stops once or twice and asks people to turn to the person sitting next to them and talk together for a couple of minutes about what they have heard so far, what questions the sermon has raised, or how it might impact their lives. The preacher can suggest a particular focus for this conversation or leave it open. After two or three minutes, the preacher invites people to conclude their conversation and continues with the sermon. Nobody is asked to speak publicly.

Stuart has often invited congregations to pause for reflection in this way. He has found that it helps to warn people at the outset that he will be doing this—in fact, just alerting the congregation that they will at some point be invited to participate quite dramatically enhances the level of engagement as people pay attention and wonder what they will be asked to do! He has also found that this is a nonthreatening way of breaking the grip of the monologue. Very few people are reluctant to talk to the person next to them, whom they often know well, and usually the only difficulty is getting people's attention again when it is time for the sermon to resume. He does sometimes give people the option of not participating, inviting those who would rather not do so to fold their arms and avoid eye contact with the person next to them! The gentle use of humor seems to help.

Discussion and feedback

Rather more demanding is the practice of preaching for a while and then asking the congregation to break into small discussion groups to reflect on what has been said or on some questions that build on this. This takes longer than pausing for reflection with one other person and, if feedback is invited, it requires at least some of the congregation to speak in public. The onus is also then on the preacher to engage with the feedback and incorporate this into the learning process, rather than just moving on to the next point.

As with the previous practice, it is possible to offer exemptions to those who would rather not participate. Some people really enjoy group discussions; others hate them. And it may be helpful to ask each group to choose a representative who is willing to speak publicly on their behalf when the time for feedback arrives. In situations where few are confident to speak in public, group leaders may be arranged ahead of time to ensure that each group has someone willing to do this.

Opportunity for comments

There are various ways of concluding a sermon—inviting people to respond, praying for the congregation, leading into a song, or simply stopping. Depending on the subject matter, another possibility is to invite comments and questions. There may be things you have said that need further explanation. Some may want to ask questions about how to respond or how to apply what you have said to their own context. Others may want to challenge some aspect of the sermon or offer another perspective. A story or example that illustrates a point from the sermon can be a helpful contribution, as can a pertinent testimony.

> **George Lings reports on a visit to Explorers Christian Church in Sydney, Australia:**
>
> They decided from the start that there was to be the crucial role of discussion, debriefing and a search for application immediately following the teaching in the meeting. They freely allow the expression of divergent, and even unorthodox, opinions yet they have found so far that this has never been confrontational or adversarial in practice. I was astonished at what I observed. Chaired by the leader of the meeting, not the speaker, many people put up their hands to make a comment, but the content did not turn into two-way talkback with the speaker. Others took up the development of what became a conversation of several threads, punctuated with a lot of laughter and a quality of comments that modelled openness, honesty and some vulnerability . . . The whole process spoke of, and taught the value of, a search for integrity, not a neat formula . . . Here was a simple way of focussing issues in discipleship and being candid about partial progress down that road. Of the fifty-five minutes of adult time, the discussion occupied twenty.[6]

6. George Lings, *Simpler Church*, Encounters on the Edge 32 (Sheffield: The Sheffield Centre, 2006), 17–18.

It can be helpful to invite people to pause for a few moments before making comments or to talk together briefly in small groups to formulate good questions or to discover if more than one person is thinking along similar lines. This can help with the quality of questions and comments. It also gives the preacher a short break before engaging with them.

Some churches invite people to engage in this process in mid-week groups, rather than at the end of the sermon. They provide summaries of the sermon, questions for discussion, and further resources. This can be very helpful and indicates a concern to build a learning community and to engage responsibly with sermons. It also allows more time for people to digest and reflect on what they have heard. But this approach lacks the immediacy of inviting questions and comments at the end of the sermon, when what has been said is still fresh in people's minds. And the preacher cannot, of course, be present at most of the midweek groups. A combination of these approaches is worth considering.

In many North American churches, adult Sunday school offers an opportunity to discuss the sermon shortly after it has been preached. This second meeting (unfamiliar in British churches) is not always used for this purpose, but it can function as a "sermon response class." A friend of ours convenes such a group in her church with the specific aim "to not waste the sermon"! Sometimes the person who has preached the sermon participates, too.

Invitation to interrupt

In some contexts it can be helpful to create an ethos in which the preacher is happy to be interrupted in mid-flow. Stuart usually invites people to do this when he is teaching, and more often than not this invitation is acted upon. In the church in Oxford that Sian pastored, interruptions were common—some of these more helpful than others! Encouraging this kind of interaction alerts the preacher to anything that has been unclear, indicates that people are engaging with the sermon, may offer perspectives that enhance learning, and can help the preacher respond to pressing concerns.

Stuart has occasionally asked someone in the congregation to interrupt him at a certain point, raising objections to what he has been saying. Although this is somewhat artificial (and can be quite worrying for a congregation until they realize it is preplanned), when a preacher is exploring a controversial issue, this can be a very effective way of reminding everyone that it is acceptable to disagree with one another but remain friends. It can lead into a dialogue in which areas of agreement and disagreement can be spelled out clearly and memorably.

Dwelling in the Word

Stuart discovered, during a visit to Pennsylvania in 2009, a group of Mennonite churches using an approach they called "dwelling in the word." Members of the community (this is practiced in a conference setting as well as in local churches) are invited to spend time quietly reflecting on a biblical passage that will shortly be the basis for a sermon. Somewhat like the monastic practice of *lectio divina*, they listen carefully for words and phrases that the Spirit draws to their attention. They then share with their neighbor how they have responded to the passage, and their neighbor then reports on this to two or three others.

This practice has a number of benefits. It prepares people to listen more attentively to the sermon and to delve more deeply than usual into the biblical passage on which it is based. It encourages everyone to participate actively and to take responsibility for learning and offering insights to others. It teaches people to listen well to each other and to share what they say succinctly. And it reminds us all that ultimately it is God's Spirit who teaches us.

> Phill Vickery recalls organizing a preaching series at Cranbrook Baptist Church in which a team of four took responsibility. They met together to plan the series, received some training, supported each other, and held each other accountable. One sermon in the series involved three of the four preaching together.

Prepare sermons together

Even if the sermon is to be a monologue, preparing to preach can be multivoiced. One way of doing this is to invite a small group to meet in the week before the sermon is due, to reflect together on the theme or biblical passage, to suggest ways of approaching this, to contribute illustrations and stories that might be helpful, to discuss how best the preacher might communicate, and to consider ways of inviting others to respond. In some churches where this is practiced, the group already knows who will be the preacher; in others the preacher emerges out of this preparation. A further possibility is to ask the congregation to suggest subjects for future sermons.[7]

It is possible to involve the whole congregation in preparing for a learning opportunity. If everyone knows in advance what the theme of a sermon will be or which biblical passage will be explored, they have time to reflect on this. Many churches publish a program of this kind, especially if they are working through a teaching series, so it should not be too difficult to provide some additional resources to help those who want to prepare in advance to do so. This approach not only helps to create a learning ethos in the church. It also equips people to engage with the sermon at greater depth and to make good use of opportunities for interaction.

☙

All the above practices are ways of enhancing the learning potential of sermons rather than alternatives to the sermon. They have learner-oriented, multivoiced and open-ended features. But some communities might want to replace at least some sermons with other ways of teaching and learning. These include:

• Interactive Bible studies, seminars, or workshops between sermons that enable people to study themes and passages in more depth.

• Interviews with guests or members of the community who have expertise on certain subjects or experience to share. Sian remembers a powerful example of this when she

---

7. On this, see June Alliman Yoder, Marlene Kropf, and Rebecca Slough, *Preparing Sunday Dinner: A Collaborative Approach to Worship and Preaching* (Scottdale: Herald Press, 2005).

visited the Willow Creek Community Church in Chicago and heard an interview with a man who had lost his wife, daughter, and mother in a road accident caused by a drunk driver. His reflections on the thorny issue of suffering formed the whole of the teaching period in that meeting.

Tim Foley recalls an occasion on which he adopted a more interactive approach:

Rather than craft a twenty-minute sermon, I designed a thirty-minute Sunday morning workshop. This made my role "facilitator" rather than "preacher." It did not take less time than sermon preparation, as thought had to be given to how best to involve people, to put them at their ease and encourage them to participate. There were several stations in the room, with people invited to move from station to station every few minutes. Each station had a facilitator to introduce a topic and invite reflection and discussion. For people tired of words, there was paper and colors were provided.

• Formal or informal debates with a skilled chair, in which different perspectives are presented and the community is invited to contribute questions and comments and to form their own judgments.

• Teaching sessions to which two or three speakers contribute, dialoguing with each other as they explore various subjects. This is a practice the annual Spring Harvest events in the UK have modeled over many years in their morning seminars, although not in their evening celebrations.

Trevor Withers reports that the "sermon" on one Sunday in his church consisted of "a three-way conversation between the three leaders on how we connect with God. This highlighted our different approaches to God and our relationship with him and gave the church an insight into how we worked together as a team."

• Invitations to members of the community to bring issues with them on which the community can engage in theological reflection. This is quite demanding on those who facilitate such reflection, but it ensures that the church is engaging with issues that members of the community are facing.

• Invitations to several members of the community to bring short contributions on a designated theme. While we were writing this book we took part in a multivoiced weekend conference organized by the Anabaptist Network and the Northumbria Community, in which there were no sermons or long lectures but many prepared contributions on an agreed theme. Feedback from participants was enthusiastic.

But we need to expand our horizons further. All the practices we have considered so far are still oriented toward those who learn best through words, whether they are listening to presentations or contributing to discussions. Such people are *auditory learners*, whose learning preference is through what they hear. Others, however, are *visual learners*, who learn best through what they see, or *kinesthetic learners*, who respond better to physical activities and learn by doing and experiencing. Learning in most churches is very heavily weighted toward auditory learners, and the practices we have suggested, although they may help auditory learners learn more effectively, do not address this issue. Given that only a third of people are auditory learners, according to current research, we are either disadvantaging two-thirds of our members or auditory learners are disproportionately represented in our churches. This is either a pastoral issue or a mission issue, or both.

We know we are in danger of oversimplifying a complex issue (some researchers identify at least seven learning styles, rather than three), but we need to start somewhere if we are to redress this imbalance and build inclusive learning communities. We also need to take care not to exaggerate the problem. These are learning *preferences*. All of us actually use all these learning styles. But we do have preferences that impact our capacity to learn and the enjoyment we find in learning. A starting point might be for a church to try to find out which of the learning styles are preferred by which of their members.

Jonny Baker describes two services at Grace, an alternative worship community in West London. Both were based on psalms and emerged from a group planning process.

In the first we had identified about ten different themes such as praise, lament, anger, despair, storytelling. Then the whole text of the psalms was printed out at different places/stations in the church along with activities or small rituals that related to the psalm and connected it with contemporary experience. These ranged from an online confession, Post-it notes of thanks, wrapping yourself in a duvet to read Psalm 91. The service involved a corporate reading of a couple of psalms sandwiched around time to walk around and pray and interact with all of the stations that had been set up. It was a powerful service, engaging with a lot of Bible text. For the second service people were invited to create their own psalm using any media they liked, and the service consisted of those being read/shown/performed. Not everyone created a psalm, but a lot did. The results were stunning and in a range of media—VJed psalms, rewrites of existing psalms that related to an urban context, and so on. Artists' gifts came to the fore. Some of it was actually great contextual theology.[8]

Margaret Cooling is an educationalist who has worked with many churches. In her very helpful book, entitled *Creating a Learning Church*,[9] she provides extensive resources to help us improve teaching and learning in our churches. Toward the end of the book she lists activities that churches can use to communicate more effectively with learners who have visual and kinesthetic preferences. These include (for visual learners) banners, art, video, displays, artifacts, demonstrations, symbols, diagrams, and activities that spark the imagination; and (for kinesthetic learners)

---

8. In his article, "Throwing a Hand Grenade in the Fruit Bowl" at www.anabaptistnetwork.com/node/356.

9. Margaret Cooling, *Creating a Learning Church* (Oxford: Bible Reading Fellowship, 2005).

participation in drama or mime, role-play, responsive storytelling, handling objects or information, taking part in learning games, celebrations, gestures, and rituals. We commend this book as a rich resource for those who want to explore multivoiced learning.

Trevor Withers gives an example of learning style preferences:

One of our church members is an artist who finds it difficult to "talk in straight lines" and cannot write notes, so found it difficult to communicate with us. With a bit of coaching and helping her to produce notes in picture form she has made some stunning contributions.

Our hope is that some readers will be quite excited by now, eager to experiment with at least some of these ideas. But others may be daunted by the challenge, unsure whether they have the time or talent to invest in such activities, reluctant to move away from the familiar, whatever its limitations. And some may have serious objections—we have heard many of these as we have presented these proposals in various places, and we promised earlier to address them before the end of this chapter. So in the final section we consider what is involved in developing a multivoiced learning community and whether this is worth pursuing.

But first, a brief word on technology.

- Are there ways in which data projectors, mobile phones, church websites, social media, and other technological resources can help? Do we embrace their potential or resist their influence? How do we decide?

- Do we encourage people to switch their phones on when they arrive so they can text immediate responses to the sermon that appear on a screen while the preacher is still speaking?

- Does posting sermons on the church website encourage discussion of what has been said or diminish their impact?

- PowerPoint is used so often (and often so badly) that many are weary of it, but can it be used well?

These questions are barely scratching the surface and new forms of technology will no doubt have appeared by the time this book is published.

But maybe we can find a place of orientation on such issues from a surprising source—the Amish, a traditional rural community with roots in the sixteenth-century multivoiced Anabaptist movement. The Amish sometimes seem to outsiders to be inconsistent, as they embrace some forms of technology but reject others in an apparently arbitrary way. In fact, a deep principle underlies what appears on the surface to be inconsistent. When considering whether to make use of technology, the Amish ask: "But does it build community?" Will this technique, this tool, this device, this process enhance the life of our community, or damage it? Technology is not inherently evil or good, but neither is it neutral. What impact will it have on the way we live and relate to one another? Maybe that is the question we need to ask as we consider the role of new technologies in the learning community.

Building a learning community

Objections to what we are suggesting are sometimes concerned with practicalities (does this actually work?) and sometimes with principles (should we do this anyway?).

The principled objections usually relate to one or more of the following concerns:

- God has appointed preachers and teachers in the church, whose ministry will be diminished if multivoiced learning is embraced.

- Multivoiced learning endangers the orthodoxy of the church, opening it up to heretical ideas and wrong interpretations of Scripture.

- It is crucial that people have certainty on doctrinal issues and clear boundaries on ethical issues, which open-ended approaches threaten.

• What seems to be a monologue is in essence a dialogue as preachers engage with the biblical text and the congregation.

• There are other opportunities for multivoiced participation, so there is no need to adapt or reduce the frequency of monologue sermons.

Add to these the objections we noted earlier, which also questioned the wisdom of this approach, and those who would oppose this strategy have many reasons to discount what we are proposing. It is unlikely that we can say anything here that will persuade those who have objections in principle to the kind of multivoiced learning we are advocating. But we insist that multivoiced learning is consistent with the witness of Scripture, has been practiced by churches in many generations, honors the contributions of sermons and the ministry of preachers, trusts the work of God's Spirit in the Christian community, and fosters discipleship rather than dependency. Furthermore, most heresies and aberrant biblical interpretations can be traced to authorized preachers, rather than to congregations empowered to become learning communities, and many Christians today find certainty and fixed boundaries much less helpful than many church leaders seem to think.

The concerns about practicalities are numerous. Here is a sample:

• Preachers have been trained to deliver monologue sermons, not to facilitate multivoiced learning, so we don't have the skills.

• Allowing interruptions, questions, and discussion breaks the flow and diminishes the sense of "anointing" preachers experience.

• People might ask questions that preachers cannot answer, which will diminish their authority.

• Congregations are not familiar with multivoiced learning and may not adapt well to such changes or welcome them.

• Multivoiced learning can be characterized by simplistic and literalistic biblical interpretation, can degenerate into a "pooling of ignorance," or can play into the hands of those who have an axe to grind.

• Inviting many people to participate reduces the quality of the teaching and may be off-putting to newcomers.

• Changing the layout and seating arrangements will be necessary if people are to discuss what they hear as well as listen.

• Facilitating multivoiced learning takes much more time than preparing a sermon and requires constant creativity.

Ben Lucas, a former student of Sian's and now a Baptist minister in Dorset, UK, wrote his dissertation on "preaching with dialogue." He has experimented with various forms of interactive learning in his church and has encountered problems. In particular, the quality of responses to the sermons has been disappointing and opportunities to participate can become an "extroverts' playground." But he has not given up. He writes:

> I have found that giving time for preparation, announcing the subject the week before, or allowing discussion time in groups before feeding back to the whole church, seems to lead to more and more voices being heard.

We should not underestimate the challenges involved in building a multivoiced learning community. This will take time and perseverance. Initial results and feedback from the congregation may be discouraging. Many churches are locked into monologue preaching and are deeply threatened by anything different.

However boring the congregation finds the sermons, however little impact they make, sermons are at least safe, familiar, and undemanding. Multivoiced learning is none of these things. Congregations will need to be trained, equipped, nurtured, encouraged, and reassured if they are to become learning communities. Gentle and honest feedback on all forms of participation will be essential if the community is to learn how to learn.

Tim Presswood wrote to us:

I often tell the story of the occasion when we were still struggling to maintain a "proper church" in a "proper church building." Clare and Deborah had taken the children out to do their activities and one or two people were absent, so I ended up with just our church secretary. I asked him whether he wanted me to deliver the sermon I had prepared and he, inevitably, responded yes. So I preached my sermon at one person!

Those who have embarked on this journey report that they have needed to press through early discouragements and invest time in helping the church learn how to learn. But this is, after all, the calling of those who exercise leadership in the churches—"to equip his people for works of service,"[10] not performing all the works of service themselves. And in time a multivoiced approach can become normal, rather than exceptional, so that reverting to a monovoiced approach becomes problematic.

One of the crucial elements in this process is embracing and constantly reinforcing the shift from performance to learning. The question asked over many Sunday dinner tables—"What did you think of the preacher today?"—is no longer the most important question. The important question is "What did we learn as a community this morning?" If there was a sermon, the preacher's contribution remains significant, but the emphasis is elsewhere.

And if our concern about multivoiced learning is that members of the congregation may be unskilled at interpreting Scripture or applying it responsibly (not that theologians and preachers are immune to such deficiencies), rather than colluding with biblical illiteracy we might offer resources and training to equip people with

---

10. Eph 4:12.

the necessary skills. This was the approach of the Lollard teachers as they circulated resources to help their "reading circles" explore Scripture together, and of the Anabaptist leaders who disseminated their "biblical concordances" to help congregations make connections between different parts of the Bible. So we have been encouraged by the appearance while writing this book of a new course, "H+," developed by the Bible Society in the UK and designed for just this purpose. This is a basic course on hermeneutics, equipping would-be biblical interpreters with the necessary skills, and focusing on the virtues required for faithful interpretation and application.

Marg Hardcastle writes:

Our congregation uses interactive "sermons" increasingly often. About three out of four sermon slots have open questions and invitations to comment. However, once a month we have a "proper" sermon. Well, we try to—the thing is that people have become so used to contributing that it is difficult not to let them, even when the invitation isn't made. Sometimes I will say: "I have prepared a sermon for you this week so I will be doing all the talking!" It doesn't always work though!

But if there are challenges for congregations in the transition to multivoiced learning, the challenges preachers face are not inconsiderable. As the objections above indicate, many feel insecure, ill equipped, and discomforted by the prospect of inviting others into the process of preparing sermons, or being interrupted and questioned during or after their sermons, let alone developing forms of learning for visual and kinesthetic learners. And most preachers prefer monologue sermons. Not only is this safer, it also feels more satisfying, more fulfilling, more "anointed." Putting it bluntly, preacher satisfaction takes precedence over congregational learning and development. And some feel threatened by the prospect of a learning community that is no longer so easy to lead and control.

After the furor that erupted when it became clear that not all evangelicals subscribed to the "penal substitution" theory of the atonement, a symposium was organized to explore the theological issues and allow both sides of a sharp debate to engage with each other. Stuart was invited and was given assurances that this really would be an opportunity for dialogue rather than lots of speeches. It wasn't. The only space for extended conversation was in his seminar, when he spoke for less than ten minutes in order to free up the rest of the hour for dialogue. Monovoiced church instincts and a concern to control the process turned even a symposium (literally a "drinking party") into a series of monologues.

On the other hand, many preachers are aware that monologue sermons are not delivering what they hope, that the effort they put into preparing and preaching them does not seem to be repaid, and that our cultural context means that sermons are uncongenial. We have been surprised and encouraged by the receptivity of many preachers and church leaders to what we have said about multi-voiced alternatives. Discovering the biblical basis for multivoiced learning and various historical precedents may then be enough to persuade some to explore this further—even if this means learning new skills, investing more time in unfamiliar practices, journeying with the congregation into the unknown, and inviting the criticism or even derision of colleagues.

And some who do take the plunge find that multivoiced learning is fun! Unpredictable, demanding, scary, risky, but full of new discoveries and unexpected outcomes. There is still scope for monologue sermons—sometimes this is the appropriate medium. But the range of possibilities is so much wider now.

6

Multivoiced Community

One another

The many "one another" or "each other" texts in the New Testament lend themselves to a series of Bible studies or sermons, as many churches know. Congregations are encouraged to reflect on their responsibilities to and for one another as, week by week, different but overlapping aspects of Christian community life are explored.

Some injunctions are quite general and are repeated several times. The most common of all is "love one another."[1] Four times the early Christians are instructed to "encourage one another"[2] and three times to "greet one another."[3] Most other phrases appear only once, although "forgive one another"[4] and "bear with one another"[5] both appear twice. But many of them

---

1. John 13:34; 15:12, 17; 1 Thess 4:9; Heb 13:1; 1 Pet 1:22; 3:8; 4:8; 1 John 3:11, 14, 23; 4:7, 11–12; 2 John 1:5.
2. 2 Cor 13:11; 1 Thess 4:18; Heb 3:13; 10:25.
3. Rom 16:16; 1 Cor 16:20; 1 Pet 5:14.
4. Eph 4:32; Col 3:13.
5. Eph 4:2; Col 3:13.

are slightly different ways of saying similar things: "be devoted to one another"[6] and "be kind and compassionate to one another"[7] are variants on the theme of love. "Live in peace with each other,"[8] "live in harmony with one another,"[9] "agree with one another,"[10] "accept one another,"[11] and "have fellowship with one another"[12] all seem to refer to similar attitudes and commitments. Similarly, "honor one another,"[13] "have equal concern for each other,"[14] "serve one another,"[15] "submit to one another,"[16] and "clothe yourselves with humility toward one another"[17] all encourage ways of relating that exclude self-centeredness and pride.

Other injunctions are expressed negatively rather than positively: stop passing judgment on one another,[18] don't bite and devour one another,[19] don't provoke and envy one another,[20] don't lie to one another,[21] don't slander one another,[22] and don't grumble against one another.[23] Evidently, the early Christians were far from perfect and needed to be challenged on various behaviors that were damaging their communities. These challenges give greater

---

6. Rom 12:10.

7. Eph 4:32.

8. 1 Thess 5:13.

9. Rom 12:16.

10. 1 Cor 1:10.

11. Rom 15:7.

12. 1 John 1:7.

13. Rom 12:10.

14. 1 Cor 12:25.

15. Gal 5:13.

16. Eph 5:21.

17. 1 Pet 5:5.

18. Rom 14:13.

19. Gal 5:15.

20. Gal 5:26.

21. Col 3:9.

22. James 4:11.

23. James 5:9.

substance to the more generalized positive injunctions, spelling out what love, encouragement, and fellowship mean in practice.

And then there are "one another" texts that are more specific. Jesus challenges us to do what he did for his disciples: "wash one another's feet."[24] James tells us to "confess your sins to each other" and to "pray for each other [to] be healed."[25] Peter tells us to "offer hospitality to one another."[26] And whoever wrote the letter to the Hebrews encourages us to "spur one another on toward love and good deeds."[27] Congregations do not always give as much attention to these more specific and more demanding "one another" texts, but they are practices that help build multivoiced communities.

Finally, there are a handful of "one another" texts that refer to the multivoiced practices we have examined in the previous chapters. Paul assures the Christians in Rome, whom he has not yet visited, that they are "competent to instruct one another" and not dependent on visiting teachers or apostles.[28] He tells the church in Colossae to "teach and admonish one another,"[29] vital practices in a learning community. We will reflect further on the role of admonition in this chapter. In Ephesians there is a phrase that points us back to multivoiced worship—"speak to one another with psalms, hymns and songs of the Spirit"[30]—and in 1 Thessalonians Paul uses a phrase that echoes his instructions in 1 Corinthians 14 about multivoiced worship—"build each other up."[31]

Many of these are well-known and much-loved texts. We read them, nod in agreement at what they require, and renew our commitment to live like this. Maybe our familiarity with them and the sheer number of references to "one another" obscures their significance. For

---

24. John 13:14.
25. James 5:16.
26. 1 Pet 4:9.
27. Heb 10:24.
28. Rom 15:14.
29. Col 3:16.
30. Eph 5:19.
31. 1 Thess 5:11.

what we have here is *the persistent rhythm and heartbeat of multivoiced community*. We are not lone pilgrims struggling with temptation, discouragement, misunderstandings, and setbacks, but companions on the journey. These texts insist that we need each other, we are responsible for each other, we are accountable to each other, and we grow as disciples through our relationships with each other.

> John Bunyan's famous *Pilgrim's Progress* is wonderful in many ways but dangerously individualistic. J. R. R. Tolkien's *The Fellowship of the Ring* has a more biblical resonance in this respect as the band of brothers puts into practice many of the "one another" texts as they urge each other on toward the goal.

The multivoiced church vision is not restricted to worship and learning. In this chapter we will explore its implications for community building, pastoral care, and encouraging one another to live as disciples of Jesus.

As we do this, we must continue to ponder the role of leaders in the churches. For just as church leaders have too often in the areas of worship and learning disempowered their congregations and adopted a monovoiced stance, many have also in the areas of pastoral care, disciple making, and community building usurped responsibilities that belong to the whole community. This creates unhealthy dependency in the congregation and, especially if the church grows, places intolerable burdens on the leaders themselves. Some church leaders behave in this way because they desperately need to be needed; others because they do not trust the work of the Spirit in the community; many others because they were trained to operate like this. We are still living with the consequences of the Christendom shift, which silenced and disinherited the laity and centralized power and ministry in the hands of the clergy.

Most of the "one another" texts make no mention of church leaders. They encourage all members of the community to take responsibility for each other and for the health of the community as a whole. Occasionally leaders do feature, at least in the verses around these texts (Peter enjoins younger people to submit to their elders as an example of the humility expected of all disciples; James suggests the church elders are invited to pray for those who are sick alongside other members of the church who are praying for one another[32]). But nowhere are church leaders given sole responsibility for pastoral care, encouraging discipleship, or building up the community.

> Many years ago when it was becoming fashionable for churches to set up "home groups" to encourage prayer, Bible study, and more interactive pastoral care, an Anglican priest experimented with this for several months before deciding it was too exhausting. He had set up a dozen such groups in his church but had decided he needed to be present at all of them every time they met to make sure nothing went wrong!

And yet church leaders play a very significant role in the New Testament. They are to be respected, supported, and honored. Nothing we have written here or in previous chapters should be interpreted as implying that leaders are extraneous or unimportant. The gift of leadership may be only one among many other gifts, but it is a crucial gift. Multivoiced churches need skilled, sensitive, godly, and effective leaders. But what they do not need are leaders operating in a monovoiced way.

In relation to community building and pastoral care, what multivoiced churches need are leaders who can broker and encourage "one-anothering." Equipping church members to fulfill this calling more faithfully, establishing pastoral care teams to respond to crises, offering their experience when required, knowing when to draw in people with particular expertise, developing processes and setting up systems to ensure nobody is

---

32. 1 Pet 5:5; James 5:14.

marginalized, providing feedback on progress, keeping a watching brief on what is happening—there is plenty for leaders to do. But the challenge, as with multivoiced worship and learning, is to unlearn monovoiced instincts and embrace a different kind of leadership.

In Christ Church, Deal, there is no recognized "pastor," and pastoral care involves the whole community caring for one another and practicing "experts-by-experience" pastoring, similar to the support encouraged in therapeutic communities. Anyone with a pastoral need is encouraged to identify someone in the community they feel safe with and meet with them. Community members are encouraged to tell their own story and to offer help from their own experience. There are leaders in the community with professional expertise, but they provide training workshops and occasional "sessions" to equip people for this multivoiced pastoring rather than taking responsibility for addressing all the pastoral needs.

The rule of Christ

Nowhere is this kind of leadership more essential than in situations where relationships have become strained, behavior has been inconsistent with the gospel, and the integrity of the community is under threat. As we have seen, several of the "one another" texts are phrased negatively, revealing the struggles the early Christians faced in their attempts to build Christian communities. Churches are imperfect communities of recovering sinners. We let each other down. We behave badly. We fall out with each other. We hurt others and ourselves. We need practices and processes which will guide us in these situations.

And we find such practices and processes scattered across the New Testament as Jesus and his disciples offer guidelines for communities that screw up but want to find ways of resolving issues. The classic passage, sometimes known as "the rule of Christ," is found in Matthew 18:

If a brother or sister sins, go and point out the fault, just between the two of you. If they listen to you, you have won them over. But if they will not listen, take one or two others along, so that "every matter may be established by the testimony of two or three witnesses." If they still refuse to listen, tell it to the church; and if they refuse to listen even to the church, treat them as you would a pagan or a tax collector.[33]

This is a frustratingly brief passage! The four-stage process that Jesus spells out is clear enough: one-to-one conversation, taking a witness, telling the church, and exclusion from the community. But it raises so many questions:

- What does "sins against you" mean? What offenses are covered? How serious do they need to be? How persistent? Where is the boundary between ethical issues and cultural preferences?

- Does the "sin" need to be against you personally, or is any "sin" damaging to the brother or sister involved and to the integrity of the community and therefore a matter for concern and action?[34]

- Who do you take with you at the second stage? Why? For whose benefit is this extra person?

- How do you "tell it to the church"? How does the church respond?

- How long do you allow at each stage before proceeding to the next? How many conversations do you have? How do you know if the person has listened at any stage?

- What does it mean to treat someone as "a pagan or a tax collector"? And is this the final outcome, or is the way open for restoration to the community?

---

33. Matt 18:15-17.

34. There is a textual issue here. Some manuscripts omit "against you," suggesting the process has a wider remit.

Insight on some of these issues can be found in other New Testament passages, in which we see the process at work in various churches and are given more detailed guidelines.[35] But many of the questions remain, and these are best addressed within communities that commit themselves to this process and to learning together how to practice it.

Uncertainty about how to apply the principles is by no means the only reason why most churches avoid this process. We live in an individualistic culture and this kind of mutual accountability is decidedly countercultural. We are members of a supposedly "tolerant" society and this process seems worryingly judgmental. We have heard horror stories of attempts to practice "church discipline" which have been abusive and have exacerbated the difficulties a church was already experiencing. We are fearful of confronting others in the way this process advocates and anxious about how they might respond. We have not been trained to do this and we are not confident our church will cope with the demands it will place on our relationships. And what is the point if our brother or sister can avoid the issue by transferring membership to the church down the road?

And yet this is how Jesus, according to Matthew, tells us we should respond when a brother or sister is behaving in ways that are contrary to the gospel and are causing pain in relationships. This is another "one another" practice. And it is clear from the rest of the New Testament that the early churches practiced this process and that the apostles taught and commended it and gave further guidance on its application.

Absent from the passage in Matthew 18 is any reference to church leaders. Presumably, if the process reaches the third stage and the church needs to be informed, the leaders will at least be involved in facilitating this, but the process Jesus lays out is multivoiced. We are responsible to and for one another. As far as possible, things are kept "just between the two of you." Others are drawn in only if the process stalls. This is one reason why the term "church

---

35. For example: Rom 15:14; 1 Cor 5:1-5; 11:28-31; 2 Cor 2:6-8; Gal 2:11-14; 6:1; Phil 4:2-3; 2 Thess 3:14-15; 1 Tim 1:20; 5:19-20; Titus 3:10.

discipline," which is often used to label this process, is unhelpful. Only at the third stage is the church as a community involved, and there is nothing to suggest that church leaders should exercise disciplinary control over the community.

But when multivoiced communities became monovoiced communities, this process was transmuted into an oppressive exercise of clerical power. Not only did the clergy assume exclusive responsibility for dealing with sins in the church; they were also able to call on the empire to enforce their decisions. Throughout the Christendom era "church discipline" was institutional, punitive, and sometimes lethal. Although some of those who exercised this power, including the medieval inquisitors, undoubtedly believed they were acting to save souls and restrain heresy and immorality that were endangering the church, there is little in this story to encourage us to restore this process. Some of the most famous church leaders succumbed to the temptation to exercise power in this way.

> Augustine of Hippo, in his struggle with the Donatist movement, infamously bequeathed to future generations an interpretation of the text "compel people to come in"[36] that resulted in untold misery for future generations of dissenters. John Calvin, too, as he attempted to build a disciplined Christian community in Geneva, authorized punitive measures that have left a stain on his reputation.

Members of the multivoiced renewal movements that we encountered in earlier chapters suffered at the hands of the inquisitors and representatives of the imperial church. Their response, however, was not to shun this process but to explore ways of restoring it as a multivoiced practice. The Waldensians encouraged members of their communities not to confess to a priest but to one another. Those who were baptized as Anabaptists committed themselves in

---

36. Luke 14:23 NRSV.

that ceremony to receive "fraternal admonition" from one another. For early Baptists this was a feature of the covenant that bound members of the church together. In light of centuries of misuse, it is not surprising that these movements made mistakes. At times, this process was applied unwisely and harshly, causing division and pain, usually because it had reverted to a monovoiced practice. The house churches that appeared in the latter part of the twentieth century in Britain and elsewhere made a further attempt to restore this practice, but again failure to ensure this was an authentically "one another" process resulted in what became known as "heavy shepherding." The experience, good and bad, of these various movements is a helpful resource for churches today that choose to restore this practice.

But is it worth it? We appreciate that there are many disincentives—we have listed some of them in this chapter. So maybe we need to consider the alternatives. What happens in imperfect communities if we do not work through this process when things go wrong? An alternative to confronting issues and attempting to resolve them is pretending they do not matter and sweeping them under the carpet. Some of the "one another" injunctions above indicate that we should not quickly take offense or step in too hastily, but this does not mean we allow issues to remain unresolved and relationships to suffer. Eventually, if we keep sweeping issues under the carpet, we will trip over the bumps. Churches that do not practice this multivoiced process are in danger of becoming unattractive and unhealthy communities, in which gossip and factions thrive, relationships are strained and broken, and pastoral care becomes firefighting. Members of such churches are left to struggle on their own with sin and failure, instead of receiving the admonition and encouragement we all need to be faithful disciples.

So we suggest that, despite all the flawed examples, disincentives, questions, and fears, the process that Jesus spells out is essential. We need each other if we are to stay on the path of faithful discipleship, especially in a culture that lures us into other ways of living and thinking. And we need ways of restoring relationships when we hurt each other.

This process is actually all about restoration. The goal, at every stage, is to resolve issues and bring about reconciliation and restoration. The context of the passage in Matthew's Gospel makes this clear. Immediately before the "rule of Christ" is the parable of the lost sheep, which is all about restoring those who have wandered from the path. Immediately following it is the parable of the unmerciful servant, in which the disciples are urged to offer unlimited forgiveness to those who have sinned against them. So we can answer at least one of the questions we posed earlier: there may be times when exclusion from the community is required, but the way is always open for restoration.

How might a church begin to practice this multivoiced community-building process? In the previous chapters we explored multivoiced approaches to worship and learning. The practices we discussed can be introduced gradually as churches experiment with various approaches and reflect on their experiences. Implementing "the rule of Christ" requires a different strategy. Unless the church understands what is involved and agrees to adopt this process, attempts to practice it will result in serious problems. The horror stories we sometimes hear that discourage us from exploring this subject any further are usually the result of churches (or more often church leaders) trying to practice this process within a community that neither understands how it works nor has agreed to operate in this way. A crisis has arisen and action is taken, but the community has not been prepared for this and its leaders have not been trained to guide the community through the process. No wonder this process is so often badly managed and causes so much pain!

It need not be like this. Before a crisis arises, churches can talk together about the kind of community they want to be, study the New Testament teaching on this subject, reflect on the questions this raises, think through the practicalities, and agree on ways forward. Only rarely will the latter stages of the process be needed if members of the community learn to practice the early stages. And as we give and receive admonition and encouragement in this way, we slowly become the kind of community that can be trusted, when necessary, to implement the latter, more challenging, stages of the process with grace and maturity.

A church in Yorkshire, UK, agreed that they wanted to practice this process. They wrote out the passage from Matthew 18 on a poster and placed this on the wall of the building in which they met, together with a commitment to implement this process when issues arose that needed to be resolved.

Community and friendship

Of course, multivoiced community is about much more than how we engage with one another when things go wrong—although it is not about less than this. So why have we addressed this issue first and at such length? Because it is a classic example of the drift into monovoiced church and the damage this causes. Because it is not often discussed and is one of the more challenging aspects of building a multivoiced community. And because any church that takes this seriously will have to investigate other forms of multivoiced community if this process is to work properly. The way this process works is a barometer of the health of the community.

One of the reasons sometimes given for not implementing this is that church members in situations calling for "the rule of Christ" to be applied can so easily leave and join another church nearby. This may be true, but such easy transfers raise serious questions about the depth and quality of relationships in our churches. The process described in Matthew 18 assumes that friendships in the community are so important that there is every incentive to resolve issues rather than losing these relationships. If we can without regret transfer membership to another church to avoid working through this process, this indicates that the community has not fostered the kinds of relationships that are essential for the process to operate effectively anyway.

Institutional membership is not sufficient. Involvement in the church that revolves around roles and responsibilities is not enough. Superficial relationships that are often all that is implied by the term "fellowship" will not do. Multivoiced community is built on genuine friendship and a level of mutual commitment that embodies the "one anothers" we looked at earlier in this chapter. One of the first questions recorded in the Bible is Cain's "Am I my brother's keeper?"[37] As much an insolent challenge or defensive plea as an authentic question, the Lord does not directly answer this question. But the rest of the Bible (and not least the "one another" texts) makes it very clear that the answer is "Yes!" We really are responsible to and for one another, as brothers and sisters, as friends.

One of the reasons given by those who leave churches (usually for other reasons than the imminent application of "the rule of Christ") is that they have not experienced authentic friendships.[38] One of the motives behind many emerging churches is the search for these kinds of relationships—a search that is sometimes rewarded and sometimes disappointed. And one of the main factors in people coming to faith in Christ and joining churches (in fact, the overwhelmingly important factor) is friendship. But monovoiced churches are often not well equipped to foster and nurture such friendships.

This was not such a problem in the past. When churchgoing was expected or required, a monovoiced approach ensured that church services were conducted, the rites of passage were provided, and the institution was respected with only minimal demands on church members. The emphasis was on worship, not community. Many of those who attended knew one another as neighbors, work colleagues, or friends anyway, so the church did not need to foster community. Three or four generations ago, when many church buildings were not only places of worship but centers of education, social care, entertainment, and the local community, friendships were fostered through a wide range of sporting, social, cultural, and philanthropic activities. But today church members are often geographically dispersed, do not meet except at church "meetings," look elsewhere for activities that the church once provided, and invest less time in relationships with other church members.

---

37. Gen 4:9.

38. Stuart has written more on this subject in Stuart Murray, *Church after Christendom* (Carlisle: Paternoster, 2005), 39–56.

Some are content with this level of involvement, and some churches cater to (or collude with, depending on our perspective) this form of belonging. Some monovoiced churches can offer a very professional service with high-quality music and outstanding preaching, excellent programs for children, and facilities for adults, all delivered in a time frame that is strictly controlled and with no expectations that those who attend will contribute in any other way than perhaps financially. The popularity of such churches, and their ability to attract newcomers, challenges our advocacy of multivoiced churches, especially when many multivoiced churches show fewer signs of growth.

However, the number of church members who drift away from the churches in search of friendship, the mission challenge of the endemic loneliness in our fragmented culture, and the instability of monovoiced churches once their charismatic preacher or worship leader moves on, all raise questions about the wisdom of investing too heavily in what may prove to be a legacy of the past rather than a harbinger of the future. Multivoiced churches may be more demanding and less polished, but they may be better equipped to nurture the kinds of friendships that might be crucial for our future.

And building multivoiced communities may be demanding but it is not complicated. It involves encouraging, facilitating, and persisting with opportunities for people to share life together. Multivoiced worship and learning can help, but friendships are likely to grow through eating together, relaxing together, engaging in projects together, traveling together, working together, praying together, laughing and crying together, helping each other out, sharing ideas and dreams, wrestling with unresolved questions of faith, visiting each other's homes, and the many other things that friends do together. And it means not being so busy with church activities and programs that friendships cannot flourish.

Friendship, we believe, is fundamental to multivoiced community. But those Jesus called his "friends" were his disciples,[39] those who had responded to the call to follow him. So in the final

---

39. John 15:15.

section of this chapter we will explore the significance of multi-voiced church for discipleship. But first, another brief foray into the world of technology.

Using the same Amish-derived question we proposed in the previous chapter—"Does it build community?"—we need to ask whether modern technological tools and processes help foster and nurture authentic friendships or hinder these.

- Do mobile phones help us to keep in touch and share life with others in ways we could not do otherwise, or do they interrupt our conversations and reduce our capacity to be fully attentive to those we are with?

- How does email communication affect the way we relate to others?

- Facebook and other social media use the language of "friends," but does this demean the term or expand its significance?

- And can virtual community enhance, supplement, or substitute for flesh-and-blood community in the way some Internet-based churches suggest?[40]

We offer these as genuinely open questions. Our own experience is that technology can both hinder and enhance community building, so our plea is for discernment and ongoing conversation.

Communities of disciples

Facebook users have "friends"; Twitter users have "followers." It is interesting that these two hugely popular social media (or at least they were when we were writing this book) have unwittingly chosen New Testament terms that highlight vital aspects of Christian discipleship. Disciples are those who follow Jesus, who have embarked on a journey of learning and discovery; and disciples

---

40. For an introduction to this issue see Mark Howe, *Online Church? First Steps towards Virtual Incarnation* (Cambridge: Grove, 2007).

are those who enjoy friendship with Jesus, which takes disciple-ship out of the realm of rules and into the realm of relationship.

The language of "friends" and "followers" may be common to contemporary social media and the New Testament, but there are, unsurprisingly, important differences. Followers of Jesus model themselves on his life, imbibe his values, embrace his priorities and commit themselves to his purposes in ways that would be unthinkable, and unwise, for those who follow others on Twitter. And one of the marks of those who follow Jesus is that they are friends with people who are different from them, breaking down social, ethnic, age, and cultural barriers, extending hospitality to all kinds of people, living out the reconciling power of the gos-pel. It was this that their contemporaries found so disturbing and yet so attractive about the early churches. At their best, churches today continue to foster these surprising and mutually enrich-ing friendships. Multivoiced communities value diverse accents and languages, the high-pitched enthusiasm of children, the frail voices but wise words of the elderly, the stumbling contributions of the less articulate, and the measured tones of those who refuse to dominate the conversation but know how to pull the threads together.

Discipleship is a perennial concern in the churches and it is evi-dent from conferences, books, articles in journals, blog comments, new initiatives, and many recent conversations that it is becom-ing a hot topic once again. Replacing the question "What do we mean by church?," which energized us in recent years but of which many of us are now weary, is the increasingly insistent clamor for fresh perspectives on discipleship. What do we do if thousands of sermons, hundreds of sparkling worship services, a plethora of Christian resources, and multiple courses and programs are not making disciples? It is here, we believe, that monovoiced expres-sions of church prove woefully inadequate.

So it is encouraging that a number of multivoiced approaches have begun to surface. If we can resist the temptation to pack-age and market these, and instead understand their dynamics and appropriate these sensitively in many different contexts, we may discover some of the resources we need. There are already, worry-ingly, several books exploring "new monasticism" and this emerg-ing movement might be swamped by popular acclaim before it matures and can offer its insights and experiences to the wider church. But this attempt to draw on the riches and wisdom of the monastic traditions, and the reception it has received, suggests that would-be disciples recognize the need to find new rhythms, disciplines, and companions if we are to be faithful followers of Jesus in a culture that is moving away from gospel values. Within the monastic traditions we find not only rich liturgical resources, personal disciplines, spiritual classics, and centuries of experience, but also appreciation of the significance of friends and compan-ions—spiritual directors, mentors, "soul friends," and relation-ships of accountability.[41]

Companions on the journey are also crucial in the recovery of catechesis that many are advocating today. Catechesis, as noted in a previous chapter, was the discipling process through which new believers were inducted into the faith and into the church. It was a lengthy and demanding process that involved instruction, renun-ciation of old ways of living, progress in understanding and prac-tice of the new faith, and regular conversations with a sponsor/companion. Many of the outstanding teachers and theologians in the early church were catechists, engaged in conversational rather than rhetorical teaching. Some form of catechesis today offers the prospect of those who join the churches being much more thor-oughly equipped to handle Scripture responsibly, apply their faith to all aspects of their lives, and participate actively in multivoiced communities.[42]

---

41. For a helpful introduction, see Jonathan Wilson-Hartgrove, *New Monasticism: What It Has to Say to Today's Church* (Grand Rapids: Brazos, 2008).

42. Many Catholic churches now use the "Rite of Christian Initiation for Adults." See also Alan Kreider's essay, "Baptism and Catechesis as Spiritual Formation" in *Remembering Our Future: Explorations in Deep Church* (ed. Andrew Walker and Luke Bretherton; Milton Keynes: Paternoster, 2007).

Other multivoiced and friendship-based approaches to discipleship are apparent. Some, like the popular *Alpha* and *Emmaus* courses, straddle evangelism and discipleship. This overlap is likely to be increasingly necessary in post-Christendom societies, but further resources will be needed for those who want to continue on the journey. Accountability groups and circles of accountability are also becoming more popular, as individualism gives way to relationships of mutual support. Many cell churches provide a measure of mutual accountability as well as opportunities for multivoiced learning, worship, and pastoral care. The Lifeshapes material, developed by the St. Thomas Crookes church community in Sheffield, UK, encourages participants to join "huddles" and advocates that these function with "high accountability, low control." And the Inspire Network, which draws on historic Methodist practices, offers another recent example of this approach to discipleship. Members of this network belong to "fellowship bands" in which they hold one another accountable.[43]

And some are discovering that discipleship and mission belong together, using the term "communitas" to describe the more intense form of community that those engaged in mission activities together experience, and recognizing that such experiences can result in significant spiritual growth.[44]

Any or all of these initiatives, and others, can be embraced by churches concerned about making and sustaining disciples. But if other dimensions of church life remain stubbornly monovoiced, this may be problematic. Those who have experienced the vitality of multivoiced approaches to disciple making may quickly become impatient with monovoiced gatherings.

Our underlying concern is that monovoiced churches tend to create dependency rather than making disciples. And this simply will not do in the contemporary environment, in which we are bombarded on a daily basis by all kinds of ideas, values, presuppositions, assumptions, challenges, and expectations that are rooted

---

43. See http://inspire-network.org.uk/network-fellowship_bands.
44. For example, Alan Hirsch, *The Forgotten Ways* (Grand Rapids: Brazos, 2006).

in a different understanding of the world from the story the Bible tells. The pressure is on for us to collude and conform. Catechesis and disciple making are not restricted to the churches.

We will not be able to resist this insidious pressure by ourselves—we will need the support of fellow disciples in multivoiced communities. And the support we need from these communities is not protection from our culture or dependency on experts offering ready-made answers to all possible questions, but opportunities for reflection with one another to help us develop the skills and resources for countercultural discipleship.

In our complex and evolving culture, no preacher or church leader, however gifted, has all that we need. Those who have expertise in biblical interpretation and who have been theologically trained bring precious resources to the community, but we cannot expect them to be experts on the diverse social, economic, political, scientific, cultural, family, neighborhood, organizational, and ethical issues we face. Theologians pontificating on scientific or economic issues they barely understand are no more edifying than scientists or economists with little or no theological education sounding off about theological matters. What we need, if we are to develop creative and thoughtful responses to the many issues that confront us day by day, is the shared experience, knowledge, expertise, and wisdom of the whole community.

> Graham Cray, who is the Archbishops' Missioner and leads the Fresh Expressions team, describes ours as a "disciple-making culture." Mennonite missiologist Wilbert Shenk, speaking several years ago at a Gospel and Our Culture conference, warned that our society was "catechizing" us, especially through films and television.

---

45. Graham Cray has also written recently: "perhaps the greatest challenge facing the church in the West is the question of discipleship" in his essay "Thus Far and Much Further: The Contemporary Scene" in *Pioneers 4 Life* (ed. David Male; Abingdon: Bible Reading Fellowship, 2011), 23.

The subtitle of *Engaging the Powers*, the final volume of Walter Wink's trilogy on the language of power in the New Testament, is "Discernment and resistance in a world of domination." In his writings he explores what he calls "the domination system" (what the New Testament often means by "the world") and how disciples of Jesus might engage with this. This powerful and pervasive system of values, institutions, forces, structures, and ideologies will mold our thinking, constrain our imagination, corrupt our morals, and dull our consciences unless we see it for what it is and develop strategies to counter its malign influence. And for this we need multivoiced churches operating as communities of discernment and resistance.

As we were drafting this chapter, serious riots were taking place in several cities across England, one of these just down the road from our home in Bristol. We heard politicians, psychologists, police officers, community leaders, and media pundits offering their views on why this was happening and what needed to be done.
· How can the churches respond?
· Do we have anything distinctive to offer?
· Who do we have in our congregations who can help us interpret this situation and think about how we might engage with it?
· How can we avoid simplistic and one-sided reactions?
· What does discernment and resistance mean in this context?

What might this mean in practice? It might mean social workers in the church (or doctors, teachers, farmers, office workers, bus drivers . . .) meeting to help one another reflect on issues they encounter in their sphere of work, perhaps resourced by those with theological expertise but limited understanding of the issues and of the social work environment. It might mean the congregation watching television advertisements together, deconstructing them, discerning the values and expectations they are promoting, and learning to engage with such catechizing mechanisms and, where appropriate, resisting their influence. It might mean addressing current issues not through well-meaning but often bland sermons but by inviting members of the church with relevant experience to share their insights and learn from one another.

In the next chapter we will continue to investigate the role of discernment in multivoiced churches. Our concern here is to underscore our need for communities in which we are not merely instructed what to believe, how to behave, and what our response should be to any and every situation. This promotes dependency rather than discipleship. There is, of course, an essential role for biblical exposition, pastoral exhortation, and uncompromising proclamation. But this may be too inflexible and generic to help us in specific situations unless we also have opportunities to draw on the insights of others in the community and reflect together on these situations. Without these we may pay lip service to what we hear but in practice simply rely on our own judgment. Monovoiced churches may incubate unhealthy dependency or breed lonely independence; they are not well equipped to make and sustain disciples.

Authentic Christian discipleship is characterized neither by heroic independence nor by unreflective dependency. We need to develop multivoiced processes and practices that avoid these pitfalls and instead promote interdependent communities of discernment and resistance. Which takes us back to where we started this chapter—the "one anothers" that tell us to eschew isolation, warn us against relying on omnicompetent leaders and invite us to welcome interdependence.

7

Multivoiced Discernment

Discerning and deciding

All communities need to develop and agree on processes for making decisions. In families, social clubs, community groups, businesses, partnerships, and organizations, as well as churches, decision-making practices need to be established and accepted. The processes may be more or less formal, written or unwritten, fixed or flexible, but ways of making and owning decisions are vital if the community is not to stagnate or disintegrate. Much of the time these processes work well, are of interest only to officeholders, and are taken for granted by most members of the community. Leadership in the community connects with decision-making processes in two ways: the processes set out the responsibilities of appointed leaders and hold them accountable; and those leaders supervise the processes and make sure they are functioning effectively.

Decision-making practices come under scrutiny when communities undergo significant transitions, which may require different ways of operating, when community leaders fail to respect them or apply them properly, or when difficulties arise for which the processes prove inadequate.

While writing this chapter, Stuart was involved in helping the table tennis club to which he belongs revise its rules and constitution. A fairly simple document had served the club well over several years but had not been adequate when a serious dispute arose between the club committee and one of the club coaches. Changes and clarifications were needed to forestall similar problems arising in the future.

Some communities, especially those influenced by various forms of anarchism, have tried to operate without such processes and without any recognized leadership. Some emerging churches have been attracted by this approach as they explore ways of relating to a postmodern culture. However, the track record of such attempts has not been encouraging. If there is no recognized leadership and there are no established decision-making processes, decisions will still be made and leaders will eventually emerge anyway, but often without the accountability that all communities need to ensure wide ownership of decisions and to protect the community from leadership abuses.

Some years ago two members of an emerging church that had tried to function without recognized leaders told Stuart what had happened. While this community was still young and quite small some new people joined them who took a different view of leadership. In fact, they decided they should become its leaders! The church had no process in place to deal with this situation or any way of resisting it without revisiting their initial decision to have no leaders.

So are churches to make decisions in the same way as other communities? Should they have rules, bylaws, and constitutions that they can refer to when disputes arise or they are exploring new possibilities? Are similar leadership structures and decision-making processes appropriate? Our experience is that there are

actually numerous similarities between the decision-making processes of churches we know and those operating in other organizations in which we have been involved. We recall meetings of the
local residents' association we belonged to in Oxford that were
almost indistinguishable from a typical Baptist church members'
meeting, except that there was no opening or closing prayer.

Maybe this is not surprising. After all, churches are made up
of members who belong to other communities and organizations,
or who have experience with decision making in their workplaces,
and it is understandable if we import or happily accept similar
processes in the churches. Indeed, some decision-making processes in other contexts may have much to teach us about participation, listening, transparency, accountability, and ensuring that
decisions are properly implemented.

But, however much we might be able to learn from the ways
other communities reach decisions, we will also want to reflect
on the teaching of Jesus and the experience of the early churches.
What did Jesus teach about leadership? One of the haunting
phrases in his teaching is "Not so with you."[1] Challenging his disciples who were arguing about who was the greatest, Jesus insisted
that leadership in the Christian community was not based on the
same values or principles as they were familiar with elsewhere.
What conclusions did the disciples draw from this? What can
we learn from the practice of the churches we encounter in the
New Testament as they resolve disputes and reach decisions? It
will come as no surprise to anyone who has read this far that we
believe the teaching of Jesus and the practice of the early churches
point us in a multivoiced direction.

One very obvious, but fundamentally important, point is that
for Christian communities *deciding* should not be separated from
discerning. Whatever form of leadership we adopt and whatever
decision-making processes we embrace, the task of the church is to
discern "the mind of Christ." This phrase appears in 1 Corinthians
2:16 at the end of an extended discussion about the role of the Spirit

---

1. Matt 20:26.

and the difference between "the wisdom of this age" and the principles that should guide the church. Paul concludes with a confident assertion that we can discover "the mind of Christ"—not, surely, a guarantee of infallibility, but an encouragement that we are not left to our own devices. Opening and closing meetings in prayer, in which we ask for divine guidance, may be an inadequate acknowledgment of this task, sometimes little more than a pious formality, but this at least points us toward this extra dimension.

So the question we need to ask as we explore New Testament teaching and practice is not just who makes decisions and how, but who is involved in discerning "the mind of Christ" and how. Monovoiced churches tend to answer both questions by affirming the role of designated leaders. They are the ones to whom the community looks for discernment and decisions. The community accepts that they have special access to "the mind of Christ" by virtue of their theological education, ordination, vocation, spiritual maturity, charismatic gifting, representative role, or some combination of these factors. Some leaders expect their congregations to trust and follow them without question or demur; others invite discussion and welcome feedback, introducing a multivoiced element. But discerning and deciding are functions of leadership.

Is this how the early churches operated? Stuart has encouraged many groups over the past twenty years to investigate this by studying two passages in the book of Acts. These are Acts 6:1-7 and Acts 15:1-22. The first passage recounts how the church in Jerusalem responded to an issue that had pastoral and administrative dimensions and was beginning to cause relational problems in this young but rapidly expanding community. The second tells the story of the "council of Jerusalem," called to resolve a dispute between those who insisted Gentile converts should adopt many aspects of Jewish law and culture and those who were determined not to impose these burdens on them. The first passage involves an issue in a single congregation; the second explores an issue affecting many communities. These passages have both pastoral and missional dimensions.

Groups are invited to study these passages together, sharing their insights, and to reflect especially on three questions:

- How were decisions made in these situations?

- What was the role of the leaders in the community?

- Do you have any reservations about the outcomes?

The third question, which discomforts some people, assumes that Luke's account of these incidents is accurate but does not assume that the early churches were perfect. They were undoubtedly attempting to put into practice what they had learned from Jesus, reflecting prayerfully on the questions and drawing on biblical resources, but these were demanding and disputed issues. Did they discern and decide well? Are there any aspects of what they decided and how they went about this that we have questions about? Rather than adopting a wooden approach to these passages and assuming the early churches always got things right, can we regard them as conversation partners whose experiences can help us as we face similar and quite different questions? In other words, can we embrace multivoiced discerning and deciding across the centuries?

As a further resource and additional discussion point, Stuart also explains very briefly the three "classic" approaches to church governance and asks the groups which of these seem best to reflect the discerning and deciding processes in the Acts passages.[2] These are:

- The *episcopal* model, which can be represented by a triangle, describes churches in which decisions are made by one person or by very few people and are passed down to the rest of the community.

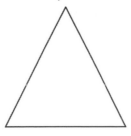

---

2. There are, of course, variants of these models and many churches do not fit neatly into such categories, but for the purposes of the exercise this simplified analysis has been adequate.

- The *congregational* model, which can be represented by a circle, is how churches understand their approach if decisions are made by the whole community meeting to discern together, or by as many of them as choose to be involved.

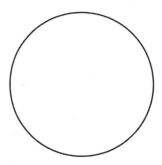

- The *presbyteral* model, which can be represented by a trapezoid, involves quite extensive consultation between members of the congregation and those who have leadership responsibility. It can be understood as a midway approach between the other two.

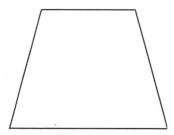

Stuart's experience over the years has been that members of the groups have interpreted these passages in different ways. Almost always there have been individuals championing each of the governance models as being closest to the pattern in Acts! No doubt our own experiences and preferences mean that we tend to interpret the passages in certain ways (and the exercise has helped participants explore and understand other interpretations), but it is also unsurprising that all three approaches have flourished and have been able to claim biblical warrant. Each has strengths and weaknesses, which the exercise goes on to tease out.

The episcopal model is clear and decisive; it allows gifted leaders to exercise their gifts; it embodies trust in those who have been commissioned to lead; it means that decisions can be made swiftly; and it releases other members of the community to concentrate on other things. However, this model places great expectations on the leaders and is open to abuse by unscrupulous, dictatorial, or insecure leaders; it does not draw on the insights and experiences of others; and communities may not own decisions which they have not been involved in making.

The congregational model is inclusive, welcoming the contributions of all members of the community; it shares power and responsibility, rather than concentrating these; and it invites ownership of decisions by those who have made them. However, this model can be time-consuming and slow; it can be less inclusive in practice than in theory if some voices are louder than others; it can fail to differentiate between the gifts and insights of different members; and it can result in conservative decisions rather than bold initiatives.

The presbyteral model, as the approach situated between the two extremes, might at its best be thought to combine the strengths of the other models. At its worst it combines their weaknesses. This model is strong on consultation and ownership; it recognizes that different decisions may need to be taken in different ways or by different people within the community. However, it is prone to becoming bureaucratic and cumbersome.

A conclusion several groups have reached as the discussion draws to a close is that most churches in practice, whatever their official governance structure, exhibit characteristics of more than one of these models. Another is that the personalities and temperaments of church leaders make a huge difference to whichever model is operating. Another still is that many churches use all three models at different times and on different issues. Monovoiced churches may tend toward the episcopal model, but actually this can be practiced in a multivoiced way. The congregational model may seem most congenial to the multivoiced approach we are advocating, but experience can prove very disappointing.

We are not arguing in this chapter for one or another of these governance models. Instead, we are suggesting that a multivoiced approach is preferable, however this is taught and implemented. And we believe that this, at least, is consistent with these passages in Acts. In both situations recognized leaders took the initiative, facilitated the process, and helped the community reach a conclusion. But the process of discerning and deciding involved many others, who talked and prayed together, shared their perspectives, and evidently owned the outcome. Acts 6:5 refers to "the whole group" participating in the process, and Acts 15:22 reports that "the whole church" commended the decision that was reached to other congregations. These passages describe multivoiced discerning and deciding in action.[3]

Struggles and resources

Why do many find the congregational model, which is the most obviously multivoiced, so often disappointing, frustrating, and thoroughly unspiritual? In our experience, many Baptist ministers are committed in principle to this model but find it deeply unedifying and unsatisfactory in practice. Many members of Baptist churches simply avoid church meetings in which decision making is on the agenda, leaving only an unrepresentative rump to make the decisions. Reacting against persistent problems with this

---

3. For readers wondering what reservations the study groups had about the decisions in Acts 6 and Acts 15, the following often emerged: Why were only men chosen in Acts 6? How did the apostles square their refusal to wait on tables with Jesus' instructions to them to wash each other's feet? And was the decision reached in Acts 15 a compromise that fudged the issue? However, most groups also acknowledged that the outcome in both passages appears to be very encouraging.

supposedly empowering but frequently debilitating process, some turn to the episcopal model or a slimmed-down version of the presbyteral model and operate in a monovoiced way. What value, after all, is multivoiced decision making if the only voices heard are complaining, raucous, oppositional, predictable, opinionated, or fearful of any changes?

We want to offer some practical suggestions in this section and point to some resources that might help those who are determined to pursue multivoiced decision making despite such discouraging experiences. But we do need first to identify some of the reasons why this is such a struggle. These include:

- *Language.* Although the term *member* can be understood organically (members of the body of Christ), it can easily convey the notion of organizational rights, so that participants in decision-making processes regard themselves as stakeholders with interests to defend and powers to exercise. The equally biblical language of *covenant* might reemphasize relationships and responsibilities and encourage us to participate in more gracious and constructive ways.

- *Ethos.* Decision-making meetings are often disconnected from the mainstream of church life. Scheduled for different times of the week, sometimes held in different meeting places or with the furniture arranged differently, they can embody a very different ethos. They present as "business meetings" and participants speak and behave very differently than if we were worshiping together, praying together, studying Scripture, engaging in missional activities, or sharing a meal together. It is surprising what impact it can have if we reconnect decision making to the life of the community.

- *Training.* Many communities assume that multivoiced decision making comes naturally or that people will pick up how to participate as they go along. Actually, this is a process that we need to learn and it requires skillful facilitation, patience, and persistence. Better still, churches need to provide training—initial training for those who are new to this process and ongoing training to enable us all to become more sensitive and more effective.

• *Focus.* Thus far in this section we have deliberately dropped the term *discerning* and focused entirely on *deciding,* whereas we consistently linked them together in the earlier part of the chapter. Did you notice? If not, you are not alone. Many churches pay lip service to discerning, but their focus is clearly on deciding. But this changes the way we participate and how we relate to each other. In fact, even focusing on making sure many voices are heard can be a distraction. Important though this multivoiced aspect is, the primary focus is to seek to discern "the mind of Christ."

> Meetings to discern and decide together in the church near Oxford in which Sian was the minister were revolutionized by the simple expedient of sharing a fish-and-chips supper together first and continuing the conversation without slipping into "business meeting" mode for the rest of the evening.

But even if we give careful attention to the issues of language, ethos, training, and focus, multivoiced discerning and deciding can be fraught with difficulties. Vested interests, strong opinions, passionately held positions, anxieties about change, divergent priorities, and wounded feelings can hinder discernment and jeopardize progress on decisions. If we are primarily interested in efficiency and accomplishing tasks, other strategies offer better prospects. Multivoiced discerning and deciding is only worth pursuing if we are equally, or even more, concerned about building community and encouraging growth in character and discipleship.

If we are not daunted by the obstacles, if we belong to a community that wants to learn to discern and decide together in a multivoiced way, some of the following resources and practices (drawn from various traditions) may be helpful.

We mentioned training just now, by which we mean a mix of information, exercises, and tools to equip communities to listen well to one another and to the Holy Spirit and to take part in discussions in ways that enhance relationships and enable good decision making. Some of the most creative and helpful resources we have come across were produced by the Baptist Union of Victoria (in Australia). *Fit4Life* contains Bible study material, role-play exercises, teaching resources, games, and reading suggestions. As churches explore these resources, understand the dynamics of relating well together and put into practice the skills taught here, the hope is that members of the community will become more self-aware, gracious, and sensitive in their interaction with each other. *Open to God* is another resource produced by the same team, offering a similar wealth of material, equipping us to engage responsibly in the process of discerning and deciding.[4] Those who have used these resources report that they are enjoyable, challenging, and transformative.

Another source of training is the range of courses run by *Bridge Builders*, for many years operating under the auspices of the London Mennonite Centre, but now an independent agency.[5] Although these primarily deal with conflict transformation, the skills they teach and the information they impart can help communities that are not experiencing conflict negotiate their way through processes of discerning and deciding without falling out with each other.

Traditions with a multivoiced heritage have developed various practices to encourage maximum participation. Some are very simple but surprisingly effective, such as:

- Passing an object around the community and inviting only the person holding it to speak;

---

4. Both resources are available (in CD format) from www.anabaptistnetwork .com.

5. For further information, see www.bbministries.org.uk.

• Asking people to spread out across the room along an imaginary straight line, taking up positions to indicate where they stand on the issue under discussion (the "conflict spectrum");

• Using sign language gestures to indicate responses to what others are saying;

• Employing role-reversal interviews or presentations, in which people present views they oppose;

• Learning how to work with the "Samoan Circle" approach that both invites participation and limits it to those within the circle of conversation;

• Simply establishing "ground rules" so that multivoiced gatherings do not become cacophonous (such as not interrupting each other, limiting the number of contributions from each person, speaking respectfully even if we disagree).[6]

The Society of Friends (Quakers) is well known for gatherings in which listening often predominates over speaking as members of the community wait for the prompting of the Spirit before contributing. For those who are unfamiliar with this practice, the silence can be disconcerting at first, but many other communities would benefit from less speaking and more attentive listening. This might help to redress the balance between discerning and deciding. Quakers also have another practice known as "clearness," in which a small group sits with someone who is in a quandary or facing a decision and they explore the issues together—not by offering advice but by asking questions to help that person discern the way forward.[7]

---

6. Further information on these and similar practices can be found in the Mediation and Facilitation Training Manual produced by the Mennonite Conciliation Service in Akron, Pennsylvania.

7. For details, see www.fgcquaker.org/resources/clearness-committees-what-they-are-and-what-they-do.

We have only experienced this "clearness" process once, but we found it helpful and will use it again in similar circumstances. We were members of a small group that sat with a close friend who had been accused of an offense. Our role was not to defend him, probe the accusations, or pass judgment, but to ask questions to help him reflect on the situation and discern how to respond and move forward.

Mennonites and other communities descended from the Anabaptist tradition advocate not only multivoiced discerning but also, wherever possible, *consensus* decision making. It is important to differentiate this from the *democratic* decision making that characterizes many other congregations. Both may be multivoiced, but the decision-making process is different. Democratic decision making ensures that, after discerning and discussing, votes are taken or some other mechanism is used to assess the mind of the meeting and to move forward in line with the view of the majority. Consensus decision making is concerned to ensure that all options have been explored, that minority views are fully understood, that those who dissent from the decision reached know that their views have been respected and consent to this decision, and that sufficient time is given to the process rather than rushing to a conclusion. This process might involve members of the community with divergent views on an issue presenting the opposing view as wholeheartedly as possible so that it is evident that each view has been fairly represented and fully understood. And consensus decision making allows for the possibility that the community might choose to adopt the perspective of a prophetic minority rather than the view of the majority.[8]

This possibility points us back in the direction of discernment. If the community's task is not simply to discuss issues and reach

---

8. In a very different tradition, the Rule of Benedict (chapter 3) commends careful attention to all voices before decisions are reached because "the Lord often reveals to the younger what is best."

decisions but to attempt to discern the leading of the Spirit, the voice of the minority may sometimes be the voice of the Spirit. This might be so even if the minority is one person. Consensus might mean recognizing that the Spirit is challenging the community to pursue a different path than the one the majority prefers.[9]

Like all communities, churches need to make decisions, some small, others far-reaching. But unlike many other communities, decision making should be preceded by discerning. Being "multivoiced" does not mean prioritizing speaking over listening; it means being open to hearing the voice of God through many different voices. The discerning church is a "hermeneutical community," in which the interpretation and application of Scripture is not the responsibility of one authorized leader or preacher but emerges from the shared reflections of many members. The discerning church values the diverse gifts of the Spirit and welcomes their contributions, weighing these carefully. The discerning church takes care to be attentive to the quieter and weaker voices as well as the more confident voices.

> In Christ Church, Deal, another practice recognized as part of the therapeutic community model is a commitment to everyone being involved in discernment and decision making. Although this can slow down the process, the church is convinced that this is essential, especially in a community in which there are many people who have been hurt by leadership that has felt abusive in previous churches or other settings. The views of newcomers are also welcome, and the church has found that their fresh perspectives can be particularly helpful.

---

9. This emphasis on discernment distinguishes consensus decision making in the Christian community from similar processes elsewhere. But the underlying principles are otherwise the same. For further resources, see www.consensusdecisionmaking.org, where the characteristics of consensus decision making are listed as follows: inclusive, agreement-seeking, process-oriented, collaborative, relationship-building, and whole group thinking. Similar principles will be familiar to anyone involved in community development: see www.cdf.org.uk.

Andrew Rollinson writes: "There is something profoundly and attractively countercultural about a group of God's people humble enough, united enough, and still enough to sense the promptings of God's Spirit in a world of fads, fashions, and formulas. True listening, like the attentiveness of lovers, requires sensitivity, awareness, patience, and commitment. It is the delicate art of discernment, not the cut and thrust of democratic processes."[10] Referring to another Mennonite practice, "shedding" (consciously owning and laying down our assumptions, preferences, and prejudices), he suggests that it is not possible to be open to the Spirit "without traveling the cruciform route of vulnerability, humility, submission, and a teachable spirit"; but he concludes: "A community of God's people genuinely open to being persuaded is a powerful instrument for God to use."[11]

This may be an attractive vision, but how does it really work in practice? Comments from some who have experienced the shortcomings and struggles involved in communities that are committed to multivoiced discerning bring a reality check. Someone familiar with Quaker practices complains about them "giving an inordinate amount of attention to an absurdly long rule book." A Mennonite friend suggests that in his tradition "process is the drug of choice." Both are concerned that the discerning phase is unnecessarily lengthy or convoluted, delaying decisions, wearying the community, and disempowering those with gifts of leadership. We need to heed these cautionary comments.

Leaders revisited

Throughout this book we have been at pains to honor those with leadership roles in the churches and to affirm the significance of

---

10. Andrew Rollinson: "The Attentive Community: Recovering God's Gift of Communal Discernment" (unpublished sabbatical study, 2009), 2.
11. Rollinson, "Attentive," p. 21. Rollinson is not, of course, claiming (any more than we are) that communities, however attentive, find discernment straightforward or should claim more certainty about knowing "the mind of Christ" than is appropriate. Discernment, he insists, is an art rather than a science.

the gift of leadership. We thank God for the many gifted and dedicated preachers, pastors, teachers, worship leaders, elders, deacons, home group leaders, administrators, priests, vicars, and ministers we know. We believe multivoiced churches need godly, creative, courageous, and effective leaders. The multivoiced practices we have described and advocated are not possible without their careful, persistent, and generous leadership. But some of the skills required to lead multivoiced churches are different from those needed in monovoiced churches (and different also from those that were prominent in whatever training most leaders received). Leading a church from monovoiced to multivoiced practices means embarking on a journey of discovery for leaders and congregation.

Some of the skills needed for leadership in multivoiced churches are being developed in emerging churches. Jimmy Long contrasts these with the characteristics he identifies as influential in inherited churches—control, command, and celebrity. Urging emerging and inherited church leaders to learn from one other, he suggests that emerging church leaders are modeling the shifts from heroic to postheroic leadership, from guarded to vulnerable leadership, from positional to earned authority, from task-oriented to community-oriented leadership, from mapping out the destination to journeying with others, from directing to empowering, and from aspiring to inspiring.[12]

As with worship, learning, and community building, so with discerning and deciding: the task of those with leadership responsibilities is neither to dominate nor to abdicate, but to facilitate. Encouraging those with valuable insights who are reticent to speak, noticing those who might otherwise be marginalized, challenging those who respond ungraciously to others, reminding those who speak a lot that listening is even more important, judging when it is time to move from discerning to deciding, summarizing the conversation and drawing out the salient points, making sure everyone knows what decision has been made and why, helping

12. Jimmy Long, *The Leadership Jump: Building Partnerships between Existing and Emerging Christian Leaders* (Downers Grove: IVP, 2009).

the community reflect on the process and learn from it—providing leadership for multivoiced discerning and deciding is multifaceted and demanding.

Nor are leaders merely process managers. Their voices, too, need to be heard if the church is to be truly multivoiced. They may offer insights, knowledge, and experience that most others do not have—theological training, experience of other churches, pastoral expertise, knowledge of the Bible and its interpretation at other times and in other places, and so on. If multivoiced processes weaken leaders there is something seriously wrong with the way we are practicing them, and the church is losing out. It is clear from the examples in Acts 6 and 15 that multivoiced discerning and deciding need not sideline church leaders. The role of the leaders in these passages is crucially important, and the respect in which they are held seems evident. In healthy multivoiced churches neither the leaders nor the community are disempowered.

Karen Stallard, now minister of Union Chapel in Islington, UK, reflecting on her ministry in a small Baptist church in East London, writes:

I am interested in how churches become "infantilized" by a church leader who acts as a "parent." As leaders take on this parenting role this silences the congregation, or makes their voices seem childish or immature and all decisions are then bounced back to the "responsible" parent who is the church leader (giving the leader more power and the opportunity for abuse). The multivoiced aspect of decision making is then lost and churches get entangled in sibling rivalry and parenting issues all being transferred during church meetings. I think I got totally embroiled in this parenting role before; now as I work at Union Chapel I am acutely aware of the need to avoid this.

One difficulty church leaders face is how to facilitate the discerning process so that many voices can be heard while at the same time contributing to the process themselves. This is especially tricky if they are chairing the meetings. The simplest solution, of course, is not to chair the meetings! Is there someone else who has the skills to do this? If there is, this can release church leaders to participate actively in the conversation. If not, the church could invite a skilled facilitator from elsewhere to take on this role. The contributions of respected leaders will inevitably carry weight—multivoiced discerning does not assume all contributions are of equal weight—but they need not overwhelm other voices.

However much we affirm the role of church leaders, though, some will be unconvinced and will find this approach to ministry uncongenial. Given the long history of monovoiced church and the accompanying leadership patterns and expectations, this is hardly surprising. And, of course, there are plenty of churches around that find the prospect of multivoiced discerning and deciding as unappealing as multivoiced worship, learning, and community building, so there is currently no shortage of ministry opportunities in this familiar mode. Our hope is that the resources we have offered here may be helpful to those who want to venture out into this alternative expression of church and ministry.

Listening to many voices

Multivoiced discernment, then, empowers all members of the community to participate in a prayerful listening and conversational process. But are there voices that we might fail to hear unless we are particularly attentive and deliberately inclusive? Encouraging multivoiced participation, creating an ethos that is conducive to this, and learning together how to share insights with each other—is this enough, or are some still liable to be excluded or marginalized?

This is a question that each community needs to ask and return to periodically, but there are some people who may often need to be welcomed into the conversation.

- How do we listen to the voices of children, whose reflections may be surprisingly insightful and whose perspectives may well be quite different from those of the adults?

- How do we ensure that the views of older members of the community are valued, especially in a culture that pays little heed to the wisdom of the elderly?

- How can we help the inarticulate and hesitant to participate without feeling embarrassed?

- Will those with learning disabilities be invited to share their ideas?

- What about those who have recently joined the community, who may not feel they have much yet to offer but who can bring fresh ways of thinking to the rest of us?

- What about the artists, sculptors, photographers, and other creative people who often struggle to offer their visual gifts in a predominantly verbal church culture?

Many of these, as we mentioned in an earlier chapter, have found opportunities in alternative worship communities that they could not find in other churches.

Phil Warburton describes the practice of the E1 Community Church:

At four vision days spread through the year we eat together and listen to each other in order to understand the direction we think God wants us to go, to look at the church finances, and to make decisions. Young people are very much included. We often feel that the spiritual lead comes from them. As an urban church there are powerful tensions, such as wealth or education, which can easily divide us. Without a multivoiced approach then these divisions may not be worked out in a healthy way.

Multivoiced discernment does not mean that all voices carry the same weight, but it does mean that any voice might be an instrument of the Spirit. So we need to listen carefully to many voices and weigh what is said.

We may find that other churches, especially those in the congregational mode, are rather surprised to receive such an invitation. Brian Haymes, a retired Baptist minister, recalls such an occasion from his days as a pastor in Exeter, UK. The congregation he served raised the question with other Baptist churches in the city as to whether their church should stay in the center, or sell the property and relocate, or develop some other physically smaller form of Christian presence in the center while starting new works elsewhere. He wrote asking for their prayers and any guidance they might give. One church replied, affirming their convictions about the presence of Brian's church in the city center. Another was not able to reply. The third let it be known that they did not think that this was any of their business. The city-center church decided to stay where it was, but Brian believes unwise independency frustrated bolder mission initiatives.

What about voices from beyond the local church? This is not an aspect of discernment for which the congregational model is well equipped. The episcopal and presbyteral models much more naturally invite voices from the wider church to participate in the discernment process and have some role in the decision making that follows this. These may be men and women with apostolic and prophetic gifts who can help us to see the bigger picture and locate our own place within this. They may be experienced church leaders who have faced similar issues before and can offer wise counsel. These voices need not be regarded as authoritative, silencing the local voices, but they can be involved in the conversation. Or we might invite other local churches to help us discern the way forward.

How much further might we go? Are there some issues, maybe many issues, on which we might invite members of the global Christian community into the conversation? Some of the decisions we make locally, especially about the use of resources, have consequences that are felt far beyond the locality. And Christians from other cultures can challenge our parochial vision and help us identify prejudices and assumptions that we might otherwise fail to notice. In the global village of the twenty-first century we can be part of a global multivoiced community.

What about voices from beyond the Christian community? There are, after all, biblical precedents for God speaking through outsiders. A classic example is the counsel given to Moses by his father-in-law Jethro, the priest of Midian, who urges him to delegate rather than wearing himself out. Jethro offers his advice and invites Moses to consider whether this might also be God's word to him. Moses receives it as such and acts on it.[13] A more amusing example is Balaam's ass, when "the LORD opened the donkey's mouth"[14] and it spoke to Balaam, who was struggling to heed what God was saying to him in other ways. Are we open to voices from beyond the church? Might we sometimes invite members of the local community to participate in our discerning and deciding process, especially if the issue is of concern to them too?

> The members of a village Baptist church were considering whether to spend quite a lot of money to upgrade their facilities. Their building was, in fact, the only community space in the village and was used by various groups. They invited village residents to join in the discussion about this issue and even encouraged them to vote when the time came for a decision to be made. No doubt contrary to the church constitution, the motion was passed by considerably more votes than there were registered church members!

If this all sounds far too complicated and time consuming, we need to remind ourselves that the bottom line is that we want to discern, as far as we are able by the grace of God, "the mind of

---

13. The full story occupies the whole of Exodus 18.
14. Num 22:28.

Christ" in relation to our situation. The process may be much less complex in practice than it seems as we spell out various aspects of it here. But listening to many voices is not about speed and efficiency. Monovoiced decision making is undoubtedly less oner-ous and many day-to-day decisions in our communities are much better handled in this way. But multivoiced discerning and decid-ing builds communities—the process is as important as the out-come—and opens us up to the surprises of the Spirit.

8

The Case for Multivoiced Church

Is it worth it?

We are enthusiastic advocates of a multivoiced approach to church life. We would not have bothered writing this book unless we believed that it is worth investing time and energy in developing multivoiced churches—planting them or transitioning them. We have explored various reasons for embarking on this journey, or pressing on in spite of setbacks; in this final chapter we will revisit these and add some further incentives.

But we have also identified various disincentives and struggles, and we have tried to deal honestly and fairly with them. So we want first to summarize these and reflect further on the challenges they present. Our hope is that setting alongside each other arguments for and against multivoiced church will clarify the issues and ensure that those who choose to embrace multivoiced practices will be under no illusions about what may be involved.

Here, then, are some of the reasons *not* to adopt the multivoiced approach we have been advocating:

- It has not been the practice of most churches over the past twenty centuries. There may be biblical warrant for it and some historical precedents, but the experience of most traditions, denominations, and congregations is that monovoiced patterns have sustained the churches over the years.

• Movements and communities that have experimented with multivoiced practices have often abandoned these in the second or third generation. If it is so difficult to sustain multivoiced church, perhaps the effort involved is not justified.

• It is too time consuming for church members. People have busy lives and cannot invest the time needed to learn the necessary skills and participate in multivoiced processes. One of the reasons for paying church leaders is to free up their time to do many of these things for us.

• It is too time consuming for church leaders. Even though multivoiced practices may eventually share the load and reduce the demands on church leaders, they are too busy to invest the time needed to introduce new processes and equip church members for multivoiced church life.

• Most church leaders have been trained to minister in monovoiced churches and many have neither the skills nor the inclination to adopt multivoiced practices or equip their congregations for this.

• Many church leaders do not believe they have congregations with the gifts, desire, or spiritual maturity to develop and sustain multivoiced practices. They may see the potential of this way of being church but, like Martin Luther when challenged to adopt a more radical and multivoiced expression of church, they do not think they "have the people for it."[1]

---

1. In the introduction to his German Mass (1526), Luther wrote: "I neither can nor may as yet set up such a congregation; for I do not as yet have the people for it."

• Multivoiced practices disempower those God has anointed and called to preach, conduct worship, provide pastoral care, and exercise visionary leadership. Multivoiced church is unsatisfying for them and deprives congregations of the ministry they should be receiving.

• Especially as communities are learning to operate in multivoiced ways, mistakes will be made, the quality of church gatherings will be variable, misunderstandings and disappointments are likely, and people may be upset and withdraw.

• Despite disclaimers, multivoiced church represents capitulation to contemporary cultural preferences, risks introducing heresies, and diminishes the authority of the churches and their authorized leaders.

• Adopting a multivoiced rather than monovoiced approach will distract attention from the primary calling of the church to participate in God's mission. Tinkering in this way reinforces the inward-looking and self-absorbed tendencies already present in many churches.

Baptist minister Ben Lucas writes:

There are times when I have instigated an interactive section of the service and I can see people physically shrink in their chairs at the prospect. Also, on a personal level, I am also aware of my own weaknesses. I worry about being put on the spot, being out of my comfort zone, being unable to chair the meeting from the front, and I also worry that something might be said by others which could be viewed as insensitive or harmful. However, I am aware that for my congregation's spiritual development (and for my own) interaction must be tried.

We have addressed most of these concerns already, so we will not repeat ourselves here or try to persuade those who are still unconvinced by the case for multivoiced church. It is important that these issues are considered carefully before setting in motion a process that will undoubtedly encounter setbacks and discouragements. Communities need to be aware of what is involved and what can go wrong if they are to press on through initial struggles and discouragements.

Later in this chapter we will pick up the last point in the previous bullet points—the missional significance of multivoiced church—and explore this in more depth than we have done so far. But first we want to reflect further on the seeming instability of multivoiced developments. As we have noted, history reveals that many movements and churches revert to monovoiced practices. Why does this happen? There are various (overlapping) explanations:

• Maybe the monovoiced default position of the mainstream church is too strong for dissident communities to resist, especially in the face of criticism.

• Maybe monovoiced church life is an inevitable aspect of movements becoming institutions. Multivoiced practices are suitable only for emerging churches.

• Maybe renewal movements develop multivoiced practices instinctively and do not establish a solid theological or ecclesial foundation for these practices.

• Maybe not enough is done to equip church members to participate, resulting in low-level contributions and eventual abandonment of multivoiced practices.

• Maybe our thesis is simply wrong—multivoiced church is not important, indeed maybe it is just another example of the dodgy practices of fringe movements.

Is there any reason to suppose that efforts to develop and sustain multivoiced churches today will be any more successful than in the past? Maybe not. But maybe our culture is more conducive to this approach now than in most previous generations. Maybe the hold of the monovoiced tradition is loosening as the mainstream churches struggle to adjust to the demise of Christendom. Maybe the financial constraints that will mean more churches will need to subsist with bivocational leaders and part-time ministry will push many into multivoiced ways of operating. Maybe we can no longer close our eyes to the limitations of monovoiced church life and our need for practices that will nurture countercultural discernment and resistance. Maybe there are enough multivoiced communities emerging in enough different traditions that we might be reaching a tipping point.

Church planter Ali Boulton writes:

Some of the difficulties that have arisen out of our multivoiced approach are demonstrated by the following comments/attitudes:
- My voice or contribution is good—others' are not so valuable;
- I don't want to hear about others' problems, mine are more significant—they moan, I share;
- If people's lives are difficult, their contributions can focus on difficulties, problems, confusion or lack of hope;
- Some people can dominate;
- People can draw unusual/unhelpful/heretical conclusions from the Bible;
- It's too intimate—there is nowhere to hide;
- Some people, sometimes, just want to be led/told rather than having to think/figure things out—multivoiced worship can be hard work!

Not all of the fresh expressions of church or emerging churches that have proliferated in the past couple of decades are multivoiced in nature, but many are. For some this has been deliberate, rooted in ecclesial convictions. For many others it has been instinctive, a natural consequence of their relatively small size, domestic setting, or inclusive ethos. As these churches grow and mature we wait to see whether they will retain their initial multivoiced approach or follow many previous movements in reverting to the monovoiced tradition.

Jenni Entrican reports that at Jacob's Well, an emerging church in Yate, UK, they make their gatherings as interactive as possible and encourage newcomers to participate. She writes:

I remember one time when we were discussing the incident of David and Bathsheba, and the most enlightened remarks came from two absolute newcomers. As a leader I've discovered that asking questions rather than providing answers stretches our minds and grows us spiritually.

There does appear to be a widespread rediscovery of smaller, simpler, more relational, and multivoiced forms of church (and not just in Western societies). Cell churches are characterized by the conviction that the cell is the basic building block of the community. Learning, worship, pastoral care, the development and exercise of spiritual gifts, witness, and service all take place in the context of these cells, with larger gatherings playing an important but supportive role. The cells are multivoiced. Those with overall leadership responsibilities in the community spend more time equipping, encouraging, reflecting, and resourcing than preaching, leading worship services, or other traditional leadership tasks. And pastoral care and discernment are dispersed.

Cell churches have also discovered that encouraging multivoiced participation in small groups empowers people to participate more actively when they gather in larger groups. Reflecting on his experience of this, Trevor Withers from Cell UK Ministries[2] sent us a list of things they had learned:

• Leadership needs to be vulnerable;

• It often helps to prime people beforehand;

• Constant encouragement is vital;

• Space for contributions needs to be intentionally created;

---

2. See http://celluk.org.uk.

- Different styles of communication should be valued;

- Warnings and explanations are helpful to those unfamiliar with multivoiced gatherings;

- Those who are facilitating meetings can ask for clarification if necessary and will try to make links with what others have contributed;

- Challenging and correcting people should normally be done in private;

- Being comfortable with silence is liberating; and

- There is no reason why multivoiced church should not be fun!

Trevor also suggests churches committing themselves to this approach should present what he calls a "theology of participation."

In other contexts we can observe similar dynamics in base ecclesial communities—small groups of Christians, most of them influenced by liberation theology, who meet regularly to study Scripture, express solidarity with each other, pray for each other, and respond together to local challenges and opportunities. In most cases these groups remain within the (predominantly Catholic) parish system, but they operate semi-independently and rely on multivoiced participation. JustChurch in Bradford, an Anglican fresh expression of church, is a recent attempt to develop a similar approach in the UK, drawing explicitly on liberation theology and operating with a highly interactive approach to worship, learning, and decision making.[3]

There are now thousands of groups in England and elsewhere that own the label "fresh expression." These vary enormously from creative missional initiatives to the rebranding of existing activities, from incarnational communities engaging with unchurched people to slightly more contemporary meetings for those who have become disconnected from more traditional churches, from

---

3. See Chris Howson, *A Just Church* (London: Continuum, 2011).

groups that will eventually be drawn back into existing church structures to planting teams that will establish new churches. There are numerous ecclesial questions to be answered over the next few years as these communities mature and wrestle with issues of identity and sustainability. But many of them are multivoiced and much less dependent on clerical leadership than previously. Whatever their structural and ecclesial future, will those who have been involved in such initiatives be content with monovoiced church in the future?

Increasingly popular, too, is the language of "simple church" to describe small groups that are intended to be easily reproducible. Allergic to the notion of growing larger or taking on institutional features, preferring instead to multiply and retain their simplicity, might these essentially multivoiced communities resist the temptation to revert to monovoiced practices? As with those identifying themselves as fresh expressions, time will tell how they develop and how sustainable they will prove to be.

All of these emerging forms of church (and others with labels such as "table churches," "household churches," "home churches," or "organic churches") have yet to demonstrate their capacity to make a significant missional impact on post-Christendom societies or their ability to thrive beyond the first generation. But many exhibit multivoiced traits—interactive learning, participatory worship, decentralized leadership, consensual decision making, and mutual accountability. Other emerging churches, especially those associated with the term "new monasticism," are more structured in their approach but also value multivoiced practices. Among the "twelve marks of new monasticism" recognized by a gathering of representatives from many groups are commitments to nurturing the shared life of the community, mutual support and accountability, and the "rule of Christ" (in Matthew 18) as the basis for resolving disputes.

In many older churches, too, multivoiced approaches are gaining ground. Not without resistance, not without setbacks and disappointments, but communities are embarking on this adventure, learning through their experiences, developing skills, and working through difficulties. A number of ministers have shared their experiences with us, reflecting very honestly and thoughtfully on the joys and struggles. One or two have found the going too tough and have given up, or at least decided to wait for a while; others are pressing on.

Is it worth the effort? We have summarized the reasons why it might not be—a daunting list. Here are the reasons why we continue to advocate multivoiced church:

- We believe that it is the biblical norm for Christian communities, derived from the teaching and practice of Jesus, modeled by the early churches, congruent with the nature of the new covenant and with the designation of the church as a "kingdom of priests," all of whom are anointed with the Spirit and gifted for ministry.

- We believe that it has been the Spirit-inspired rediscovery of numerous renewal movements that have attempted to restore biblical principles to church life, and that this pattern will continue in every generation.

- We believe that it counteracts clericalism and diminishes the danger of ministerial burnout or abusive leadership, and that it prepares churches for when they will no longer have full-time leaders.

- We believe that it enhances biblical literacy and theological acuity, equipping us to engage responsibly with issues we encounter in all spheres of life.

- We believe that it releases gifts throughout the community that can enrich every aspect of our community life.

- We believe that it has the capacity to make and sustain disciples and to develop us into communities of discernment and resistance, rather than dependent consumers and passive congregations.

• We believe that it makes a significant contribution to
the emergence of missional churches in post-Christendom
societies.

Once again, we do not intend to repeat arguments from earlier chapters. Instead, we will concentrate on the final point and
explore the relationship between multivoiced church and the
church's vocation to mission. So we conclude this section by simply inviting those who have read this far to weigh the pros and
cons of a multivoiced approach to church. Is it worth it? What do
you think?

Alan and Eleanor Kreider belong to a church that invites multivoiced
participation in a "sharing time"—an opportunity for testimonies,
community news, prayer requests, and responses to sermons. They
value this but acknowledge that in their church, and in others that
practice this, sharing time is not without problems:

At times members' contributions can be hackneyed, maudlin, self-
indulgent, and too explicit about medical issues. In some churches the
extroverted few monopolize the microphone.[4]

Multivoiced and missional

We believe that multivoiced church "makes a significant contribution to the emergence of missional churches in post-Christendom
societies." Really? But hasn't this book been about internal church
dynamics? What do these have to do with the mission of God and
the participation of our churches in this mission? Does it matter
whether the churches are monovoiced or multivoiced as long as
they are missional? Isn't this whole discussion equivalent to Nero
fiddling while Rome was burning or rearranging the deck chairs

---

4. Alan Kreider and Eleanor Kreider: *Worship and Mission After
Christendom* (Harrisonburg: Herald Press, 2011), 132.

on the Titanic as it heads toward the iceberg? Maybe we don't just need to ask whether it is worth investing time and energy in building multivoiced communities but whether this is an irresponsible distraction from the missional vocation of the church and the urgent task of discovering how to incarnate the gospel in a changing culture.

We have some sympathy with these concerns. We know how tempting it is for churches, faced with the double challenge of arresting persistent decline and making an impact on a society that seems increasingly resistant to the gospel, to invest their energies in a range of programs and strategies that promise to deliver growth and progress. Some of these may be helpful, although not if they are simply bolted on and not if they exhaust people. And we have sympathy also with the widespread advocacy of a shift from "attractional" to "incarnational" approaches to mission. This is a necessary shift of emphasis in a post-Christendom context, in which "come to church" strategies are unlikely to be effective. But we are not persuaded that these approaches should be opposed to each other or that the internal life and health of the churches can be disconnected from their missional vitality.

Of course, for some churches turning inward and concentrating on internal issues is a never-ending quest for ecclesial perfection or a way of avoiding the harder missional challenges. But for others the hope is that internal renewal and transformation will enable the church to be more effective in mission. We have written this book because we share this perspective. And we recognize in many emerging churches and in conversations with many church planters the same conviction—that it matters what kind of church emerges or is planted if this community is to be effective in mission.

We believe that multivoiced practices equip churches and their members to participate more wholeheartedly, creatively, and sensitively in the multifaceted mission of God. We suggest that these practices have the potential to make our churches more attractive (this is not the same as attractional) and help us all to incarnate and communicate the gospel in our daily lives.

Those who urge us to abandon, or at least de-emphasize, attractional forms of mission in favor of an incarnational approach rightly recognize that in post-Christendom the church is no longer at the center of society but on the margins, that "going to church" is culturally alien and unattractive to most people in this society, and that the onus is increasingly on all of us to engage in dispersed forms of mission in the various spheres of life in which we spend most of our time. Our calling is to live out, and when appropriate speak out, the gospel in our homes, neighborhoods, workplaces, and social networks.

This does not preclude the churches taking all kinds of initiatives as communities, but it has been true for some time already that most people in our society are much more likely to encounter individual Christians in the places in which they live, work, and relax than they are to respond to invitations to participate in church-run activities. And friendship over an extended period of time is the normal context within which people come to faith in Christ. As the number of people who have had no contact with the churches increases and the last generation with childhood memories of the churches disappears, encounters and friendships with individual Christians will be even more crucial.

All of which means we cannot evade the question of how our churches will equip and resource us for this dispersed long-term incarnational mission.

We return to a contention we introduced in Chapter 1: active participants in healthy multivoiced churches are much more likely to be confident in sharing their faith with others, ready to engage in social action, hospitable to their neighbors, alert to pastoral opportunities beyond the church, and able to participate in gracious dialogue with people of other faiths or none. The skills we learn in multivoiced churches are transferable to other spheres of life. The responsibility of being active participants, rather than passive consumers, will stand us in good stead as we interact with others in different contexts:

- Learning to listen without interrupting, to contribute thoughtfully and graciously to discussions, to disagree without demeaning others, to represent fairly views we dissent from, and to work toward consensus—if we can develop these attitudes and skills in multivoiced churches, we can bring these into our workplaces, clubs, and neighborhood organizations.

transfer to other settings

• Learning to wrestle with Scripture and reflect theologically on issues, rather than being spoon-fed by preachers who do all the work for us, equips us with the tools we need to grapple with issues at work and in society and to offer perspectives that challenge conventional thinking and reflect a Christian worldview.

• Learning to listen to the Spirit as the church prays and worships together and to participate in this multivoiced environment offers the prospect that we will be able to tune in to what the Spirit is saying in other environments too.

• Learning to share with the Christian community testimonies of what God has been doing in our lives and of our struggles with faith and discipleship may loosen our tongues in our daily lives and help us to share with others authentic and winsome testimonies.

• Learning to respond sensitively to pastoral needs in the congregation and to allow others to support us when we are struggling means we are more likely to be alert to pastoral opportunities with friends and colleagues and also less likely to come across as having everything "sorted" (an unattractive trait of some Christians).

There is, however, as we acknowledged earlier, an important proviso to our contention that multivoiced churches are more likely to empower and equip missional disciples for ministry beyond the church. It is essential that multivoiced does not equate to "busy." We acknowledge that some of the processes and practices we have described are more time-consuming than their monovoiced alternatives. Some of them require additional time as the church is learning them; others require more time even when they are familiar. To compensate for this, multivoiced churches may need to review and reduce their activities in order to free up time for the kinds of dispersed mission for which they are equipping their members. We suggest that this streamlining of activities is well worth considering in multivoiced *and* monovoiced churches, many of which are unnecessarily busy.

> Alan and Eleanor Kreider enthuse about the potential of multivoiced worship:
>
> The multivoiced *ekklesia* functions as a political reality, and we who are trained in it learn to function articulately in other assemblies as well. The culture of the church makes a difference. It influences the cultures of work and extended families, of civic organizations and political debate. It enables the voiceless—children, the disabled, and the inarticulate—to find their voice.[5]

Multivoiced churches are also, we suggest, inherently more attractive than monovoiced churches in contemporary culture. There may be cultural contexts in which this is not the case, but in postmodern and post-Christendom Western societies multivoiced churches present fewer obstacles to those who are journeying toward faith and involvement in our communities. There is in postmodern societies deep suspicion of institutions, structures of power and control, authoritarian leadership styles, and claims to have all the answers to all the questions anyone might ask. The churches are widely regarded as falling foul of all these strictures and as desperately, but illegitimately, trying to hold on to the status and respect they enjoyed in the Christendom era. Multivoiced churches represent a different and culturally more appropriate approach.

We need to stress again that this is not a matter of kowtowing to contemporary culture at the expense of faithfulness to Scripture

---

5. Kreider and Kreider, *Worship and Mission After Christendom*, 176.

or the tradition of the church. There are aspects of postmodern suspicion that we need to challenge, and there are aspects of church life that cannot and should not conform to postmodern ideologies and prejudices. But missional churches will do all they can to engage sensitively with their culture. And we hope it is clear by now that we are not advocating multivoiced practices primarily on the basis of their cultural congruity. We believe that they are biblical, that there are many historical precedents, that they are more effective in nurturing and sustaining disciples, and that they build healthier and more mature communities. For these reasons we would advocate them in cultures that would find them less congenial. But in contemporary Western societies the cultural context provides an additional missional incentive.

How important is it that our churches are attractive to others? We have affirmed the shift from an "attractional" to "incarnational" approach to mission as a necessary corrective in a post-Christendom society. And we have proposed that multivoiced churches equip us for dispersed, incarnational witness. But biblical evidence indicates that authentic mission is both "go and tell" and "come and see" (centripetal and centrifugal). The church is pictured as a light set on a hill as well as scattered salt. It is to be an attractive community. It may be that the attractional approach is a legacy of the Christendom era, when the church was dominant and demanded attention and allegiance, but there was much about it that was very unattractive. By contrast the pre-Christendom churches, which were socially on the margins and quite dangerous to join, were deeply attractive because of the quality of their internal life and relationships. We will need attractive, rather than attractional, churches in post-Christendom too.

Are multivoiced churches attractive to those who are exploring Christian faith and who find their way into church meetings? Some church leaders are dubious, as we noted in an earlier chapter, worried that multivoiced communities offer a less-polished performance than monovoiced churches. Returning once more to a passage we have referred to many times, 1 Corinthians 14, we find Paul concerned not only that multivoiced gatherings build up the church but also that they mediate the presence and power of God to outsiders (vv. 23-25). His counsel to the Corinthians was not that they abandon multivoiced worship in favor of more-polished services, but that they learn how to practice multivoiced worship in such a way that outsiders would encounter God in their meetings. For older people with memories of monovoiced church who are finding their way back to faith and church, perhaps a polished performance is more attractive than the multivoiced alternative we are advocating. But as post-Christendom advances, that generation passes, and these memories fade, perhaps multivoiced churches will come into their own.

Where do we go from here?

The conclusion of some who have stayed with us through this book may be that you are not convinced—either by our advocacy of multivoiced church, or that it is feasible in your context, or that it is important enough to invest the amount of time needed to bring about the changes we have described.

But for those who are persuaded and are asking the question "Where do we go from here?" we suggest that the answer depends on several factors:

- Who is asking the question;

- Who else shares your vision;

- What influence you have in your community;

- What aspects of multivoiced church are already operating in your community;

- How decisions are made about changes;

- Where progress might be made quite readily; and

- Where there is likely to be greater resistance.

In a predominantly monovoiced church the case for multivoiced church will need to be argued persuasively if there is to be any significant change of emphasis. In churches that already embrace some multivoiced processes it may be possible to introduce others and to embed this approach more deeply in the community. In communities that are already multivoiced in ethos and practice, especially churches that have emerged recently, it may be helpful to be explicit about the reasons for this and put in place strategies to counter any reversion to monovoiced practices as the community grows and ages.

Angie Tunstall, a Baptist minister working with Urban Expression, reflects:

As a healthcare chaplain with often tiny congregations of three to eight people in worship services or evening prayers it is easier for all to be involved and empowered to contribute and take responsibility. I have found empowering people to contribute to multivoiced church when leading worship in a congregation of 150 to 200+ to be more of a challenge. Albeit, I remember one morning at the beginning of the service asking people to pick up a Bible from the pew, choose very short sentences from the Psalms and speak out the words . . . we heard voices that morning never heard before . . . and probably never heard since!

In a small community it may be appropriate to celebrate publicly with those who have birthdays. Stuart had some involvement for a while with quite a large church that had introduced the practice of singing "Happy Birthday" to members when the church was much smaller. As it had grown they had continued with this practice and now sang this song almost every Sunday, often to three or four people. This was very wearying and quite inappropriate.

The size of the church is a significant factor. Some multivoiced practices are harder to introduce or sustain in larger communities. In some situations this might be an argument for reducing the size of the church by planting new communities. In others it may mean that subdivisions of the church are the context for at least some multivoiced practices. In others again it may mean making use of appropriate technology to enable more people to participate and be heard. Basic group dynamics are at work here. It is not helpful for large churches to attempt to operate as if they were small churches.

There are other significant factors too: the culture of the church, its theology, the tradition that has shaped it, the gifts and experience of those with leadership responsibilities, the maturity of the congregation and its openness to changes, the architecture and ambience of wherever it meets, and so on. As each situation will be different, we simply offer in conclusion some general guidelines:

- Some multivoiced practices are more threatening than others to churches that are unfamiliar with them. It is probably best to start at the shallow end.

- We need to ensure that people understand the rationale for these practices. This will need to be repeated and reinforced over and over again.

- It is crucial that the community owns these practices widely and deeply, so that they are not being imposed by a few enthusiasts.

- Multivoiced practices take time to learn, and we need to be patient as we explore these together and encourage persistence with what may be unfamiliar.

- If we are to make progress in these practices we will need to provide training and opportunities for feedback and reflection.

- We should anticipate setbacks, discouragements, and resistance. We should also be alert to slippage back into monovoiced practices even when we think multivoiced practices are well established.

• Church leaders need to be very clear that multivoiced processes need managing carefully, which requires considerable skill and grace, and they also mean a loss of "control," which may be disconcerting.

• Churches do not need to go it alone. It is surely appropriate for churches that are pursuing a multivoiced approach to welcome the input of other communities that are further down the road and conversations with churches that are embarking on the same journey.

The Authors

Stuart is a trainer and consultant in the United Kingdom's Anabaptist Network, which he chairs. He is also the founder of Urban Expression, an urban church planting agency. He travels widely, in and beyond  the United Kingdom, teaching in seminaries and congregations. He has written several highly acclaimed books on urban mission, post-Christendom, and Anabaptism, including the Herald Press titles *Planting Churches in the 21st Century* and *The Naked Anabaptist.*

Stuart was born in London and has spent much of his life there, initially as a student at London University, then as a church planter in Tower Hamlets, later as a lecturer at Spurgeon's College. He has two sons and two grandchildren. His doctoral research was in Anabaptist hermeneutics.

Sian was born in Scotland but grew up in Wales in a Welsh-speaking family, moving to England in childhood. After obtaining a degree in English Literature, she worked in Washington, D.C., with the Baptist World Alliance. She then returned to the United Kingdom to work with the Baptist Missionary Society, for a time as director for missionaries. She trained for the Baptist ministry at Regent's Park College, Oxford, obtaining a BTh degree. She has also trained as a spiritual director.

After marrying Stuart in 2000, Sian served as the minister of Littlemore Baptist Church, near Oxford. She is now a tutor at Bristol Baptist College. She is also moderator of the Baptist Union's Faith and Unity Department.

Stuart and Sian are members of St Mark's Baptist Church in Bristol. This is the first book they have coauthored.